INTERNATIONAL CUISINE

INTERNATIONAL CUISINE

beef, lamb, & pork

JG
PRESS

Published by World Publications Group, Inc.
455 Somerset Avenue
North Dighton, MA 02764
www.wrldpub.net

All interior photographs courtesy of Sunset Books.
Cover photograph: ©Heath Robbins/Foodpix

ISBN 1-57215-454-3

Editors: Joel Carino and Emily Zelner
Designers: Lynne Yeamans and Stephanie Stislow
Production Director: Ellen Milionis

Printed and bound in China by SNP Leefung Printers Limited.

1 2 3 4 5   06 05 03 02

contents

beef, lamb, & pork

sautéed pork with red peppers

preparation time: about 50 minutes

2 pounds boneless center-cut pork loin, trimmed of fat and cut into ½-inch-thick slices

4 cloves garlic, minced or pressed

Pepper

2 tablespoons butter or margarine

4 medium-size red bell peppers, seeded and cut into thin strips

About 2 tablespoons salad oil

¾ cup *each* dry white wine and regular-strength chicken broth

Lemon wedges

Italian parsley sprigs

1 Sprinkle pork with garlic and season to taste with pepper. Set aside.

2 Melt butter in a wide frying pan over medium-high heat. Add bell peppers and cook, stirring often, until soft (about 10 minutes). Transfer to a warm platter and keep warm.

3 Add 1 tablespoon of the oil to pan. Then add pork, a portion at a time (do not crowd pan); cook, turning once, until browned on both sides (4 to 5 minutes), adding more oil as needed. As pork is cooked, transfer to platter with peppers.

4 Add wine and broth to pan; stir to scrape browned bits free. Bring to a boil; boil, stirring often, until sauce is reduced to ½ cup (8 to 10 minutes). Pour over pork and peppers. Garnish with lemon wedges and parsley sprigs.

makes 6 servings

per serving: 345 calories, 35 g protein, 6 g carbohydrates, 20 g total fat, 106 mg cholesterol, 267 mg sodium

tequila pork chops

preparation time: 20 minutes

4 center-cut loin pork chops (*each* about ¾ in. thick)

½ teaspoon cumin seed

¼ cup butter or margarine

3 cloves garlic, pressed or minced

¼ cup fat-skimmed chicken broth

½ cup tequila

2 tablespoons lime juice

2 to 4 teaspoons minced fresh jalapeño chilies

Salt and ground white pepper

1 Trim and discard fat from chops. Wipe chops with a damp towel, then press cumin seed equally onto wide sides of each piece.

2 Place a 10- to 12-inch nonstick frying pan over high heat. When hot, add 1 teaspoon butter, tilting to coat pan. Add chops; brown well on each side, about 6 minutes total. Stir in garlic.

3 Remove pan from heat (away from a vent, fan, or inflammables). Stir broth, tequila, and lime juice into pan. Set over high heat. When liquids boil, reduce heat and simmer until meat is no longer pink in center (cut to test), about 4 minutes. Transfer chops to a platter; keep warm.

4 On high heat, boil pan juices until reduced to 3 to 4 tablespoons, about 2 minutes. Add remaining butter, in a lump, and stir until blended with sauce. Season to taste with chilies. Pour sauce over pork. Season to taste with salt and pepper.

makes 4 servings

per serving: 450 calories, 35 g protein, 1.5 g carbohydrates, 33 g total fat, 145 mg cholesterol, 230 mg sodium

butterflied beef ribeye with tapenade

preparation time: 25 minutes

1 boneless beef ribeye (prime rib) roast (2½ to 3¾ lbs.), trimmed of fat

1 jar (6 to 8 oz.) tapenade

1 teaspoon grated lemon peel

1 Make a lengthwise cut down center of beef, cutting to within 1 inch of bottom surface; then press beef open to make a butterfly shape. Make a similar lengthwise cut through each of the 2 thick sections. Pull cuts open; press beef to make it 1½ to 2 inches thick. Thread 2 long (at least 18-inch) metal skewers parallel to each other lengthwise through beef.

2 Combine tapenade and lemon peel. Rub 2 to 3 tablespoons of the tapenade mixture all over beef. Set remaining tapenade mixture aside.

3 Place beef on a grill 4 to 6 inches above a solid bed of very hot coals (you can hold your hand at grill level for only 1 to 2 seconds) or over very high heat on a gas grill. Close lid on gas grill. Cook, turning as needed to brown evenly, until meat in thickest part is done rare; cut to test (16 to 20 minutes). Thinner parts will be more done.

4 Transfer beef to a carving board. Remove skewers and slice meat. Offer remaining tapenade mixture to add to taste.

makes 10 to 14 servings

per serving: 248 calories, 23 g protein, 0 g carbohydrates, 16 g total fat, 68 mg cholesterol, 493 mg sodium

butterflied beef cross-rib with cilantro-jalapeño cream

preparation time: 30 minutes

1 boneless beef cross-rib roast (2½ to 3 lbs.), trimmed of fat

¼ cup orange juice

5 tablespoons lime juice

¾ teaspoon ground cumin

¾ cup minced cilantro

½ cup nonfat or reduced-fat sour cream

1 fresh jalapeño chile, seeded and minced

Cilantro sprigs

Salt and pepper

1 Make a lengthwise cut down center of beef, cutting to within 1 inch of bottom surface; then press beef open to make a butterfly shape. Make a similar lengthwise cut through each of the 2 thick sections. Pull cuts open; press beef to make it 1¼ to 1½ inches thick. (If necessary, cut beef lengthwise again and pull these cuts open.)

2 In a deep bowl, mix orange juice, 4 tablespoons of the lime juice, cumin, and ¼ cup of the minced cilantro; add beef and turn to coat.

3 In a small bowl, mix remaining 1 tablespoon lime juice, remaining ½ cup cilantro, sour cream, and chile. Cover and refrigerate.

4 Lift beef from marinade; discard marinade. Lay beef flat and thread 3 long (at least 18-inch) metal skewers parallel to each other lengthwise through it. Place beef on a lightly oiled grill 4 to 6 inches above a solid bed of very hot coals (you can hold your hand at grill level for only 1 to 2 seconds) or over very high heat on a gas grill. Close lid on gas grill. Cook, turning as needed to brown evenly, until meat in thickest part is done rare; cut to test (about 15 minutes). Thinner parts will be more done.

5 Transfer beef to a carving board; garnish with cilantro sprigs. Remove skewers; slice meat. Offer the sour cream-chile sauce, salt, and pepper to add to taste.

makes 10 to 12 servings

per serving: 307 calories, 20 g protein, 3 g carbohydrates, 23 g total fat, 71 mg cholesterol, 64 mg sodium

fajita sandwiches

preparation time: 30 minutes

½ cup lime juice

2 tablespoons chili powder

2 teaspoons ground cumin

1 teaspoon dried oregano

½ teaspoon ground cinnamon

About 1 pound skirt steak, trimmed of fat

¼ cup salsa

¼ cup nonfat or reduced-fat sour cream

1 large onion, cut into ½-inch-thick slices

2 large green bell pepper, seeded and cut into quarters

4 soft sandwich rolls (*each* about 6 inches long), split

1 In a large bowl, stir together lime juice, chili powder, cumin, oregano, and cinnamon. Cut steak into 4 pieces; add to lime juice mixture and turn to coat evenly.

2 In a small bowl, stir together salsa and sour cream; cover and refrigerate.

3 Place onion and bell peppers on a lightly oiled grill 4 to 6 inches above a solid bed of hot coals (you can hold your hand at grill level for only 2 to 3 seconds) or over high heat on a gas grill. Close lid on gas grill. Cook, turning vegetables to brown evenly, until vegetables have dark grill marks and are slightly limp (6 to 8 minutes for onion, 10 to 15 minutes for bell peppers). As vegetables are done, remove them from grill and keep warm, covered with foil.

4 As soon as you have removed enough vegetables from grill to make room for steak, lift steak from marinade and place it on grill; discard marinade. Cook, turning once, until meat is browned on both sides and done to your liking; cut to test (7 to 9 minutes for medium-rare). Remove from grill. Place rolls on grill and cook, turning once, until crisp and golden on both sides (1 to 2 minutes).

5 When peppers are cool enough to handle, rub off any loose bits of skin. Separate onion slices into rings. Cut steak across the grain into ½-inch-wide strips.

6 To assemble sandwiches, fill rolls with steak, onion, bell peppers, and salsa mixture.

makes 4 servings

per serving: 436 calories, 30 g protein, 48 g carbohydrates, 13 g total fat, 58 mg cholesterol, 628 mg sodium

pan-fried steaks with vermouth glaze

preparation time: about 20 minutes

1 tablespoon butter or margarine

1 tablespoon salad oil

4 boneless top sirloin or New York strip steaks (about 2 lbs. *total*), cut 1 to 1½ inches thick

1 tablespoon Dijon mustard

3 tablespoons dry vermouth or dry white wine

1 Heat butter and oil in a wide frying pan over medium-high heat. Add steaks and cook, turning once, until browned outside and still pink in center when cut (10 to 14 minutes total). Transfer to warm plates and set aside.

2 Add mustard and vermouth to pan drippings and stir briskly until hot. Spoon sauce over steaks.

makes 4 servings

per serving: 460 calories, 49 g protein, 2 g carbohydrates, 27 g total fat, 144 mg cholesterol, 256 mg sodium

lamb chops with cherries & orecchiette

preparation time: about 30 minutes

8 lamb rib chops (about 2 lbs. *total*),
  each about ³⁄₄ inch thick, trimmed of fat

12 ounces (about 3½ cups) dried orecchiette
  or other medium-size pasta shape

⅓ cup seasoned rice vinegar

1 tablespoon chopped cilantro

1 tablespoon chopped parsley

1 to 2 cloves garlic, minced or pressed

½ teaspoon ground coriander

¾ cup currant jelly

½ cup raspberry vinegar

¼ cup orange juice

1 tablespoon chopped fresh tarragon
  or ³⁄₄ teaspoon dried tarragon

1½ cups pitted dark sweet cherries

1 Place chops on lightly oiled rack of a broiler pan. Broil about 6 inches below heat, turning once, until done to your liking; cut to test (8 to 10 minutes). Meanwhile, bring 12 cups water to a boil in a 5- to 6-quart pan over medium-high heat. Stir in pasta and cook just until tender to bite (8 to 10 minutes); or cook according to package directions. Drain well. Transfer to a large nonmetal bowl and add rice vinegar, cilantro, parsley, garlic, and coriander; mix thoroughly but gently. Keep warm.

2 Combine jelly, raspberry vinegar, orange juice, and tarragon in a 1½- to 2-quart pan. Cook over medium heat, whisking, until smoothly blended. Add cherries and cook, stirring gently, just until warm. Remove from heat.

3 Spoon pasta onto individual plates. Arrange lamb chops alongside and top with fruit sauce.

makes 4 servings

per serving: 709 calories, 32 g protein, 120 g carbohydrates, 11 g total fat, 66 mg cholesterol, 481 mg sodium

hoisin-honey lamb with couscous

preparation time: 20 minutes

2 cups fat-free reduced-sodium chicken broth

1 cup shredded carrots

1 cup couscous

1 pound lean boneless leg of lamb
  (a chunk or steaks), trimmed of fat

6 tablespoons hoisin sauce

2 tablespoons honey

2 to 3 teaspoons minced fresh ginger

½ teaspoon vegetable oil

12 green onions, cut into ½-inch lengths

¼ cup cilantro leaves

1 In a 1½- to 2-quart pan, bring broth to a boil over high heat. Stir in carrots and couscous. Cover tightly, remove from heat, and let stand until almost all liquid has been absorbed (about 5 minutes).

2 Meanwhile, cut lamb across the grain into bite-size strips about ¼ inch thick. Place in a large bowl and stir in hoisin sauce, honey, and ginger.

3 Heat a wok or wide nonstick frying pan over high heat. Add oil, then onions. Cook, stirring, just until onions are tinged with brown (1 to 2 minutes). Transfer onions to a bowl.

4 Pour lamb mixture into pan; cook, stirring, until lamb is no longer pink (about 2 minutes; scrape off a little sauce to check). Return onions to pan and stir to heat through.

5 Spoon couscous mixture into a serving bowl and top with lamb mixture. Sprinkle with cilantro.

makes 4 servings

per serving: 445 calories, 31 g protein, 61 g carbohydrates, 6 g total fat, 73 mg cholesterol, 845 mg sodium

pork & apple stir-fry

preparation time: about 40 minutes

½ cup orange juice

¼ cup minced fresh mint

2 tablespoons reduced-sodium soy sauce

1 tablespoon minced fresh ginger

1 clove garlic, minced or pressed

1 pound boned pork loin or shoulder (butt), trimmed of fat

2 medium-size red-skinned apples such as Red Gravenstein or Red Delicious, cored and chopped

2 tablespoons lemon juice

1 tablespoon vegetable oil

1 small onion, cut into thin wedges

3 cups hot cooked rice

1 or 2 medium-size oranges (peeled, if desired), sliced crosswise

Mint sprigs (optional)

1 To prepare teriyaki sauce, in a medium-size bowl, mix orange juice, minced mint, soy sauce, ginger, and garlic; set aside.

2 Slice pork across the grain into ⅛-inch-thick strips about 2 inches long. Add pork to teriyaki sauce in bowl; cover and refrigerate for at least 15 minutes or until next day. Mix apples with lemon juice; set aside.

3 Heat oil in a wok or wide frying pan over high heat. Add onion; cook, stirring, until soft (about 2 minutes). Add apples; cool, stirring, until hot (about 1 minute). Spoon mixture into a bowl and set aside.

4 With a slotted spoon, transfer pork to pan; reserve teriyaki sauce in bowl. Cook, stirring, until meat is lightly browned (about 2 minutes). Return apple mixture to pan, then add any remaining teriyaki sauce and bring to a boil, stirring.

5 Mound rice on a platter. Pour pork mixture over rice; garnish with orange slices and, if desired, mint sprigs.

makes 4 servings

per serving: 497 calories, 30 g protein, 69 g carbohydrates, 11 g total fat, 67 mg cholesterol, 365 mg sodium

smoked pork chops with polenta

preparation time: 30 minutes

2 packages (about 1 lb. *each*) prepared polenta

1 small can (about 8½ oz.) cream-style corn

4 to 6 smoked pork chops (about 1¼ lbs. *total*)

About 2 tablespoons grated Parmesan cheese

2 tablespoons chopped parsley

1 With your hands, press polenta into a shallow 2½- to 3-quart baking dish, making an even layer over bottom of dish. Spread corn evenly over polenta. Place pork chops on top of corn.

2 Bake in a 400° oven until pork chops are hot in center; cut to test (about 25 minutes). Sprinkle with cheese and parsley.

makes 4 servings

per serving: 378 calories, 24 g protein, 46 g carbohydrates, 11 g total fat, 58 mg cholesterol, 2,237 mg sodium

triple corn stew

preparation time: about 35 minutes

8 ounces chorizo sausages, casings removed

1 can (about 14 oz.) yellow hominy, drained

1 can (about 17 oz.) cream-style corn

2 cups fresh-cut yellow or white corn kernels (from 2 large ears corn); or 1 package (about 10 oz.) frozen corn kernels, thawed; or 1 can (about 1 lb.) corn kernels, drained

1 teaspoon cornstarch

½ cup fat-free reduced-sodium chicken broth

Thinly sliced red radishes

1 Coarsely chop or crumble sausage; place in a 4- to 5-quart pan. Cook over medium heat, stirring, until well browned (15 to 20 minutes). Discard fat.

2 Add hominy, cream-style corn, and corn kernels to pan. Cook, stirring occasionally, until heated through (about 5 minutes).

3 In a small bowl, mix cornstarch and broth; stir into corn mixture and cook, stirring, until stew comes to a boil. Ladle stew into wide serving bowls; garnish with radishes.

makes 4 servings

per serving: 347 calories, 14 g protein, 54 g carbohydrates, 11 g total fat, 32 mg cholesterol, 752 mg sodium

red pepper mustard rack of lamb

preparation time: 30 minutes

1 cup drained bottled roasted red peppers (about one 7- to 8-oz. jar)

2 tablespoons balsamic vinegar

3 tablespoons honey

1½ tablespoons dry mustard

½ cup Dijon mustard

1 teaspoon minced fresh rosemary or crumbled dried rosemary

4 racks of lamb (13 to 16 oz. *each*), trimmed of fat, bones Frenched

1 In a blender or food processor, combine roasted peppers, vinegar, honey, dry mustard, Dijon mustard, and rosemary. Whirl just until peppers are finely chopped; do not purée.

2 Coat lamb all over with a third of the roasted pepper sauce. Set remaining sauce aside.

3 Place lamb racks, bone side down, in a foil-lined 11- by 17-inch roasting pan. Roast in a 475° oven for 15 minutes. Turn racks over and return to oven. Reduce oven temperature to 350°; continue to roast until a meat thermometer inserted in thickest part registers 140°F for medium-rare (about 10 more minutes). Or cut to test.

4 Cut racks in half or into individual chops; allow a half-rack or 3 or 4 chops for each serving. Offer reserved roasted pepper sauce to spoon over individual servings.

makes 6 to 8 servings

per serving: 249 calories, 22 g protein, 9 g carbohydrates, 11 g total fat, 72 mg cholesterol, 520 mg sodium

thai pocket bread sandwich

preparation time: 30 minutes

1 pound lean ground beef

2 medium-size red bell peppers

2 tablespoons minced fresh ginger

2 cloves garlic, minced or pressed

½ teaspoon crushed red pepper flakes

½ cup chopped cilantro

3 tablespoons peanut butter

2 tablespoons soy sauce

2 tablespoons lime juice

1 teaspoon Asian sesame oil

4 pocket breads (*each* 6 to 7 inches in diameter)

1 large tomato, sliced

8 butter lettuce leaves, rinsed and crisped

1 Crumble beef into a wide frying pan. Cook over high heat, stirring often, until browned and crumbly (5 to 7 minutes). Spoon off and discard fat.

2 While beef is browning, seed and thinly slice bell peppers. Add peppers to pan along with ginger, garlic, and red pepper flakes; cook, stirring often, until peppers are soft (3 to 5 minutes).

3 In a small bowl, smoothly mix cilantro, peanut butter, soy sauce, lime juice, and oil; add to beef mixture and stir to blend well. Remove pan from heat.

4 Cut pocket breads in half crosswise; fill equally with tomato slices, lettuce, and beef mixture.

makes 4 servings

per serving: 516 calories, 31 g protein, 45 g carbohydrates, 24 g total fat, 69 mg cholesterol, 965 mg sodium

reuben quesadillas

preparation time: 15 minutes

½ cup salsa

½ cup sour cream

2 cups shredded Swiss cheese

4 large flour tortillas (*each* about 10 inches in diameter)

3 cups packaged coleslaw mix

8 ounces thinly sliced corned beef

1 In a small bowl, stir together salsa and sour cream.

2 Sprinkle ¼ cup of the cheese over half of one tortilla. Then place ¾ cup of the coleslaw mix on cheese. Drizzle about 3 tablespoons of the salsa mixture over coleslaw. Lay a quarter of the corned beef over coleslaw; top with ¼ cup more cheese. Fold tortilla over to cover filling. Repeat to make 3 more quesadillas.

3 Place quesadillas slightly apart on a large baking sheet. Broil 4 to 6 inches below heat until crisp and lightly browned (1 to 2 minutes; watch closely). Using a wide spatula, carefully turn each quesadilla over. Broil until crisp and lightly browned on other side (1 to 2 more minutes).

4 Cut quesadillas into wedges. Transfer to plates and serve with remaining salsa mixture.

makes 4 servings

per serving: 640 calories, 34 g protein, 43 g carbohydrates, 37 g total fat, 120 mg cholesterol, 1,414 mg sodium

oven-roasted prime rib bones

preparation time: about 40 minutes

3 1/2 to 4 pounds standing rib bones

1/3 cup Dijon mustard

2 tablespoons red wine vinegar

1/4 cup salad oil

1 clove garlic, minced or pressed

1/2 teaspoon *each* dry thyme and Worcestershire

1/4 teaspoon pepper

Watercress (optional)

Pickled sweet cherry peppers (optional)

1 Trim excess fat from ribs, then place ribs in a shallow roasting pan or broiler pan. In a small bowl, whisk together mustard and vinegar. Beating constantly, slowly pour in oil. Then add garlic, thyme, Worcestershire, and pepper; beat until well blended. Generously brush about two-thirds of the mustard mixture over all sides of meat, then pierce meat all over with tines of a fork.

2 Roast in a 425° oven, turning ribs over several times and basting with remaining mustard mixture, until done to your liking; cut to test (20 to 25 minutes for medium-rare). To serve, cut into individual ribs; arrange on a warm platter and garnish with watercress and cherry peppers, if desired.

makes 4 servings

per serving: 623 calories, 30 g protein, 3 g carbohydrates, 53 g total fat, 112 mg cholesterol, 685 mg sodium

skewered beef with apple & lettuce

preparation time: about 30 minutes

1 piece fresh ginger (about 1 inch square), peeled and minced

1/4 cup soy sauce

2 tablespoons *each* firmly packed brown sugar and dry white wine

1 tablespoon sesame seeds

1 1/2 teaspoons Asian sesame oil

1 tablespoon hot chili oil or 1/2 teaspoon ground red pepper (cayenne)

2 pounds boneless beef chuck or top round, trimmed of fat and cut into 1 1/2-inch chunks

1 large apple

Butter lettuce leaves, rinsed and crisped

1 In a bowl, mix ginger, soy sauce, sugar, wine, sesame seeds, sesame oil, and chili oil. Stir in beef and let stand for 5 to 10 minutes.

2 Lift beef from marinade and drain briefly; reserve marinade. Thread beef equally onto 4 metal skewers; place skewers on greased rack of a broiler pan. Pour marinade into a small pan and bring to a boil over high heat.

3 Broil beef 4 to 6 inches below heat, turning as needed and brushing often with marinade, until browned on outside but still pink in center; cut to test (about 8 minutes). Meanwhile, core and slice apple and line a platter with lettuce leaves.

4 To serve, push beef off skewers onto lettuce. Wrap beef and apple slices in lettuce and eat out of hand.

makes 4 servings

per serving: 396 calories, 44 g protein, 11 g carbohydrates, 18 g total fat, 148 mg cholesterol, 711 mg sodium

pork with orange-cranberry sauce

preparation time: 20 to 25 minutes

4 boneless center-cut pork loin chops (about 1¼ lbs. *total***), trimmed of fat**

¾ cup beef broth

¼ cup dried cranberries

2 tablespoons frozen orange juice concentrate, thawed

1 tablespoon Dijon mustard

1 teaspoon cornstarch

2 teaspoons butter or margarine

2 teaspoons olive oil

Orange slices and thyme sprigs (optional)

1 Place each chop between 2 pieces of plastic wrap. With a heavy, flat-sided mallet, pound meat firmly but gently all over to a thickness of ¼ to ⅓ inch.

2 In a small bowl, stir together broth, cranberries, orange juice concentrate, mustard, and cornstarch. Set aside.

3 Melt butter in oil in a wide nonstick frying pan over medium-high heat. When butter sizzles, add as many pork pieces to pan as will fit without crowding (you may need to cook pork in batches). Cook, turning once, until pork is well browned on both sides and no longer pink in center; cut to test (4 to 5 minutes). Transfer to a platter and keep warm.

4 Add broth mixture to pan, increase heat to high, and bring to a boil, stirring. Then continue to boil and stir until slightly thickened (about 1 minute). Pour over pork. Garnish with orange slices and thyme sprigs, if desired.

makes 4 servings

per serving: 262 calories, 32 g protein, 10 g carbohydrates, 9 g total fat, 95 mg cholesterol, 357 mg sodium

pounded pork & chili chops

preparation time: 25 minutes

1 tablespoon chili powder

½ teaspoon ground cumin

2 cloves garlic, pressed or minced

½ cup minced onion

2 tablespoons vegetable oil

4 boneless center-cut pork loin chops (about 1¼ lbs. *total***), trimmed of fat**

2 medium-size ripe avocados, pitted, peeled, and sliced

Cilantro sprigs

Orange wedges

1 In a small bowl, mix chili powder, cumin, garlic, onion, and oil. Spread about 1 tablespoon of the chili mixture on each side of each chop. Place each chop between 2 sheets of plastic wrap. With a heavy, flat-sided mallet, pound meat firmly but gently all over to a thickness of about ¼ inch.

2 Place pork on a lightly oiled grill 4 to 6 inches above a solid bed of hot coals (you can hold your hand at grill level for only 2 to 3 seconds) or over high heat on a gas grill. Close lid on gas grill. Cook, turning once, until pork is well browned on both sides and no longer pink in center; cut to test (5 to 6 minutes).

3 Serve pork with avocados; garnish with cilantro sprigs and orange wedges. Squeeze orange juice over meat and avocado to taste.

makes 4 servings

per serving: 467 calories, 35 g protein, 14 g carbohydrates, 31 g total fat, 87 mg cholesterol, 94 mg sodium

joe's sausage & greens with eggs

preparation time: about 35 minutes

1 pound mild or hot Italian sausages,
   casings removed

1 large onion, finely chopped

2 cloves garlic, minced or pressed

½ pound mushrooms, thinly sliced

¼ teaspoon *each* ground nutmeg, pepper,
   and dry oregano

¾ pound red Swiss chard, cut into thin shreds
   (about 6 cups; keep stems and leaves separate)

4 eggs

Salt

1 cup shredded jack cheese

1 Crumble sausages into a wide frying pan; cook over high heat, stirring, until meat is well browned. Discard all but 2 tablespoons of the drippings; then add onion, garlic, mushrooms, nutmeg, pepper, and oregano. Cook, stirring often, until onion is soft and all liquid has evaporated (about 10 minutes). Stir in chard, a portion at a time, starting with stems, and cook until chard is just wilted (3 to 4 minutes).

2 In a bowl, beat eggs until blended. Add eggs to chard mixture; stir over low heat just until eggs are softly set. Season to taste with salt, then sprinkle with cheese.

makes 4 servings

per serving: 542 calories, 33 g protein, 11 g carbohydrates, 41 g total fat, 307 mg cholesterol, 1,197 mg sodium

sausage & fig grill

preparation time: about 25 minutes

4 to 8 mild or hot Italian sausages
   (¾ to 1½ lbs. *total*)

¼ cup butter or margarine, melted

1½ teaspoons minced fresh rosemary
   or 1 teaspoon dry rosemary

8 thin slices French bread

12 small or 6 large fresh figs,
   stems trimmed

6 ounces Jarlsberg cheese,
   cut into 1-inch chunks

1 Place sausages on a grill about 6 inches above a solid bed of hot coals. Cook, turning often, until meat is no longer pink in center; cut to test (about 15 minutes).

2 Meanwhile, stir together butter and rosemary. Brush bread with some of the mixture, place on a cooler area of grill, and cook, turning once, until toasted on both sides (about 5 minutes). Set aside.

3 If using large figs, cut them in half. Alternate figs and cheese on each of 4 metal skewers. Place on grill and cook, turning once and basting with remaining butter mixture, until figs are warm and cheese is soft (2 to 4 minutes).

4 To serve, transfer skewers to a warm platter and accompany with toast and sausages.

makes 4 servings

per serving: 853 calories, 38 g protein, 58 g carbohydrates, 52 g total fat, 145 mg cholesterol, 1,653 mg sodium

roast rack of lamb with potatoes

preparation time: about 45 minutes

Parsley Butter (recipe follows)

1 rack of lamb (2 to 2½ lbs.)

4 to 6 red thin-skinned potatoes (each 2 to 2½ inches in diameter), scrubbed

1 Prepare Parsley Butter and rub about 1½ tablespoons over all sides of lamb. Place lamb, fat side up, in a shallow roasting pan; insert a meat thermometer in thickest part (not touching bone). Pierce unpeeled potatoes in several places; arrange in pan beside lamb. Roast in a 425° oven until meat thermometer registers 145° for medium-rare and potatoes feel soft when squeezed (about 35 minutes). If lamb is done before potatoes, remove it from pan and keep warm.

2 To serve, cut lamb between ribs into individual chops; offer remaining Parsley Butter to top lamb and potatoes.

PARSLEY BUTTER

Mix ¼ cup butter or margarine (at room temperature), 3 tablespoons minced parsley, and 1 small clove garlic (minced or pressed). Season to taste with salt and pepper.

makes 2 servings

per serving: 1,930 calories, 65 g protein, 33 g carbohydrates, 169 g total fat, 385 mg cholesterol, 488 mg sodium

broiled lamb chops with papaya chutney

preparation time: about 35 minutes

Seasoned Yogurt (recipe follows)

¼ cup *each* sugar and cider vinegar

1 small onion, minced

½ cup raisins

1 teaspoon *each* ground cinnamon and ground ginger

1 large papaya or 3 medium-size nectarines or peaches, peeled, seeded or pitted, and cut into ¼-inch-thick slices

8 to 10 single-rib lamb chops (1½ to 2 lbs. *total*), trimmed of fat

Salt and pepper

1 large cucumber, seeded and cut into strips (optional)

1 Prepare Seasoned Yogurt; set aside.

2 Combine sugar, vinegar, onion, raisins, cinnamon, and ginger in a wide frying pan. Cook over medium-high heat, stirring often, until onion is soft and raisins are plump (about 10 minutes). Add papaya and stir gently until heated through (about 3 minutes). Keep warm. Place lamb chops on rack of a broiler pan and broil about 4 inches below heat, turning once, until well browned on both sides but still pink in center; cut to test (6 to 8 minutes). Season to taste with salt and pepper. Spoon papaya chutney mixture over lamb chops or serve in a separate bowl. Offer Seasoned Yogurt and, if desired, cucumber strips alongside.

makes 4 servings

SEASONED YOGURT

Mix 2 cups plain yogurt, ¼ teaspoon chili powder, ½ teaspoon ground cumin, 1 teaspoon sugar, and 1 tablespoon mustard seeds.

makes about 2 cups

per serving of lamb and chutney: 297 calories, 19 g protein, 38 g carbohydrates, 8 g total fat, 58 mg cholesterol, 60 mg sodium

per tablespoon of seasoned yogurt: 11 calories, 0.6 g protein, 0.9 g carbohydrates, 0.6 g total fat, 2 mg cholesterol, 7 mg sodium

black bean fillet

preparation time: 30 minutes

About 1¾ pounds narrow end beef tenderloin, trimmed of fat

¼ cup salted, fermented black beans, sorted of debris and rinsed

2 cloves garlic, peeled

2 tablespoons Asian sesame oil

2 teaspoons minced fresh ginger

FREEZING COOKED MEAT MIXTURES The fastest dinner of all is the one that's already cooked and tucked away in the freezer, just waiting for a busy day. Cooked meat mixtures such as sauces, stews, and chili are good choices for this kind of advance planning; make a double batch of spaghetti sauce or your family's favorite beef stew then freeze the leftovers. After cooking, let the meat mixture cool; then seal airtight in a tightly covered freezer container or in a plastic freezer bag.

1 Fold narrow end of beef under to make meat evenly thick. Tie snugly every 1½ inches with cotton string.

2 In a blender or food processor, whirl beans, garlic, oil, and ginger until smooth. Rub this mixture over all sides of beef.

3 Place beef on a rack in a 9- by 13-inch broiling pan. Roast in a 450° oven until a meat thermometer inserted in thickest part registers 125° for rare (about 20 minutes). Cut off and discard strings; then thinly slice beef across the grain.

makes 6 servings

per serving: 272 calories, 28 g protein, 1 g carbohydrates, 16 g total fat, 82 mg cholesterol, 351 mg sodium

malaysian satay

preparation time: 25 to 30 minutes

2 cloves garlic, peeled

1 large onion, quartered

2 tablespoons ground cumin

2 tablespoons ground coriander

1 tablespoon sugar

1 teaspoon ground turmeric

1 stalk fresh lemon grass, trimmed and coarsely chopped

2 tablespoons vegetable oil

2 pounds lean boneless beef sirloin, trimmed of fat

Salt

1 In a blender or food processor, combine garlic, onion, cumin, coriander, sugar, turmeric, lemon grass, and oil. Whirl until smooth; then transfer to a large bowl.

2 Cut beef into 1-inch cubes; add to marinade and mix to coat well. Then thread beef on five 14-inch-long metal or bamboo skewers.

3 Place skewers on a lightly oiled grill 4 to 6 inches above a solid bed of very hot coals (you can hold your hand at grill level for only 1 to 2 seconds) or over very high heat on a gas grill. Close lid on gas grill. Cook, turning as needed to brown evenly, until beef is done to your liking; cut to test (5 to 7 minutes for medium). Serve beef on or off skewers; season to taste with salt.

makes 8 servings

per serving: 222 calories, 27 g protein, 5 g carbohydrates, 10 g total fat, 76 mg cholesterol, 60 mg sodium

beef with mushrooms & madeira sauce

preparation time: about 25 minutes

1½ pounds lean ground beef; or 4 small beef fillet steaks (*each* 1 to 1½ inches thick)

1 tablespoon butter or margarine

1 tablespoon salad oil

4 diagonal slices French bread (*each* about ¾ inch thick)

Butter or margarine

½ pound mushrooms, thinly sliced

½ cup Madeira; or ½ cup regular-strength beef broth and 1½ teaspoons lemon juice

½ cup whipping cream

1 If using ground beef, shape meat into 4 oval patties, each about 1 inch thick.

2 Melt the 1 tablespoon butter in oil in a wide frying pan over medium-high heat. Add meat and cook, turning once, until well browned on both sides and done to your liking; cut to test (6 to 10 minutes for rare). Meanwhile, toast bread and spread with butter; place a slice of toast on each of 4 dinner plates.

3 Top each piece of toast with a beef patty or steak and keep warm. Add mushrooms to pan and cook over high heat, stirring, until lightly browned; spoon over meat. Add Madeira and cream to pan and boil, stirring often, until sauce is reduced by about half; pour sauce over meat and mushrooms.

makes 4 servings

per serving: 708 calories, 35 g protein, 24 g carbohydrates, 52 g total fat, 170 mg cholesterol, 336 mg sodium

zucchini-crusted ground beef bake

preparation time: about 45 minutes

1½ pounds medium-size zucchini, shredded

2 eggs

1 cup shredded mozzarella cheese

1 cup shredded sharp Cheddar cheese

1 pound lean ground beef

1 clove garlic, minced or pressed

1 medium-size onion, chopped

½ teaspoon salt

1 can (8 oz.) tomato sauce

2 teaspoons dry oregano

1 green or red bell pepper, seeded and cut into thin strips

¼ pound mushrooms, sliced

⅓ cup grated Parmesan cheese

1 With your hands, press out any moisture from zucchini. Beat eggs in a large bowl. Lightly mix in zucchini and ½ cup each of the mozzarella and Cheddar cheeses. Spread evenly in a lightly greased shallow 10- by 15-inch baking pan. Bake in a 450° oven for 10 minutes.

2 Meanwhile, crumble beef into a wide frying pan; stir in garlic and onion. Cook over medium-high heat, stirring often, until onion is soft (about 10 minutes); discard drippings. Stir in salt, tomato sauce, and oregano. Spoon mixture evenly over zucchini crust. Arrange bell pepper and mushrooms evenly over sauce. Sprinkle with remaining ½ cup each mozzarella and Cheddar cheeses; top with Parmesan cheese.

3 Return to oven and continue to bake until topping is bubbly and lightly browned (about 20 more minutes). To serve, cut into squares.

makes 6 servings

per serving: 366 calories, 28 g protein, 10 g carbohydrates, 24 g total fat, 155 mg cholesterol, 749 mg sodium

flank steak tortitas

preparation time: about 35 minutes

¼ **cup chopped garlic**

½ **cup chopped green onions, including tops**

2 tablespoons minced fresh jalapeño chilies

1 teaspoon ground cumin

**2 tablespoons fresh oregano leaves
or 1 teaspoon dried oregano**

2 tablespoons balsamic vinegar

1 beef flank steak (1½ to 1¾ lb.)

1 red onion (¾ lb.)

About 2 teaspoons olive oil

16 round or oval rolls (about 2 inches wide)

1 In a blender or food processor, whirl garlic, green onions, chilies, cumin, oregano, and vinegar until coarsely puréed.

2 Rinse flank steak and pat dry. Rub garlic mixture over meat.

3 Peel red onion; cut crosswise into ½-inch slices. Rub lightly with olive oil.

4 Cut rolls almost in half horizontally, leaving attached on one side. Pile into a basket.

5 Lay steak and onion slices on a barbecue grill over a solid bed of very hot coals or high heat on a gas grill (you can hold your hand at grill level only 1 to 2 seconds); close lid on gas grill. Cook meat, turning to brown evenly, until as done as desired in center of thickest part (cut to test), 12 to 15 minutes for rare, about 20 minutes for medium-rare. Grill onion slices, turning with a wide spatula, until lightly browned on each side, about 13 minutes. Transfer meat and onion to a carving board. Serve hot, warm, or cool.

6 Cut beef across the grain into thin, slanting slices. Tuck slices of meat and pieces of red onion into rolls.

makes 8 servings

per serving: 349 calories, 22 g protein, 35 g carbohydrates, 13 g total fat, 43 mg cholesterol, 353 mg sodium

roast ribs

preparation time: about 35 minutes

8 pounds beef standing rib bones

2 teaspoons *each* **dry rosemary, dry thyme leaves, and rubbed sage**

Salt and pepper

1 Arrange ribs in a single layer on racks in 2 large roasting pans, overlapping to fit, if necessary.

2 In a small bowl, combine rosemary, thyme, and sage; rub evenly over ribs. Season to taste with salt and pepper.

3 Roast in a 500° oven until meat between ribs is done to your liking when cut (25 minutes for rare, 30 minutes for medium). Transfer ribs to large serving platters; slice between bones.

makes 8 servings

per serving: 733 calories, 41 g protein, 1 g carbohydrates, 62 g total fat, 161 mg cholesterol, 120 mg sodium

san francisco burgers

preparation time: about 20 minutes

1½ pounds lean ground beef

Salad oil

Oyster sauce

4 thick slices sourdough or French bread

Dijon mustard

4 large butter lettuce leaves, rinsed and crisped

1 Shape beef into 4 patties, each about ¾ inch thick. Lightly coat a wide frying pan with oil; set over medium-high heat. When pan is hot, add patties and cook, turning once, until done to your liking; cut to test (about 10 minutes for medium-rare). Remove patties from pan and discard drippings.

2 Spread one side of each patty with about 1½ teaspoons of the oyster sauce; return patties to pan, sauce sides down, and cook just until glazed (about 30 seconds). Spread top of each patty with 1½ teaspoons oyster sauce; turn over and cook for 30 more seconds.

3 Lightly toast bread and place on 4 plates. Spread each slice with 1 teaspoon of the mustard and 2 teaspoons of the oyster sauce. Top with a lettuce leaf and a beef patty. Offer additional mustard and oyster sauce to add to taste.

makes 4 servings

per serving: 482 calories, 36 g protein, 27 g carbohydrates, 25 g total fat, 104 mg cholesterol, 1,056 mg sodium

borrego beef & chorizo chili

preparation time: about 45 minutes

1½ pounds lean ground beef

½ pound chorizo sausages, casings removed, meat cut into ½-inch-thick slices

1 medium-size onion, sliced

2 cloves garlic, minced or pressed

3 to 4 tablespoons chili powder

1 teaspoon *each* dry oregano and ground cumin

1 can (about 14½ oz.) diced tomatoes in purée

1 can (about 15 oz.) kidney beans

1 can (8 oz.) tomato sauce

4 to 6 cups lightly packed shredded iceberg lettuce; or 4 to 6 cups corn chips

About ⅔ cup shredded jack cheese

About ⅔ cup shredded sharp Cheddar cheese

1 Crumble beef into a 4- to 5-quart pan; add chorizo. Cook over medium-high heat, stirring occasionally, until beef is browned. Discard all but about 2 tablespoons of the drippings. Add onion and garlic; cook, stirring, until onion is soft (5 to 10 minutes). Blend in chili powder, oregano, and cumin; cook, stirring, for 1 more minute.

2 Stir in tomatoes and their liquid, undrained kidney beans, and tomato sauce. Bring to a boil; then reduce heat, cover, and simmer for 15 minutes, stirring occasionally. Line individual bowls with lettuce and top with chili. Sprinkle with jack and Cheddar cheeses.

makes 4 to 6 servings

per serving: 676 calories, 45 g protein, 31 g carbohydrates, 42 g total fat, 143 mg cholesterol, 1,185 mg sodium

veal & asparagus platter

preparation time: about 55 minutes

1½ pounds lean boneless veal,
   cut into inch-thick slices

Salt and pepper

All-purpose flour

About ¼ cup butter or margarine

About 2 tablespoons salad oil

2 pounds asparagus, tough ends removed

½ pound mushrooms, sliced

2 tablespoons brandy (optional)

½ teaspoon *each* dry tarragon and dry mustard

⅔ cup half-and-half

1 tablespoon lemon juice

1 Trim and discard any fat and membrane from veal. Sprinkle veal lightly with salt and pepper and dust with flour; shake off excess. Melt 1 tablespoon of the butter in 1 tablespoon of the oil in a wide frying pan over medium heat. Add about a third of the veal and cook, turning as needed, until well browned on both sides and no longer pink in center; cut to test (about 10 minutes). Transfer to a warm platter; keep warm. Repeat to cook remaining veal, adding more butter and oil as needed.

2 Meanwhile, in a wide frying pan, bring 1½ inches water to a boil over high heat. Add asparagus, reduce heat, cover, and boil gently just until tender when pierced (5 to 7 minutes). Drain well; arrange on platter with veal.

3 In frying pan used for veal, melt 2 more tablespoons butter over medium heat; add mushrooms and cook until lightly browned. Stir in 1 tablespoon flour; cook, stirring, for 1 minute. In a small, long-handled pan, heat brandy (if used) just until barely warm. Set aflame (not beneath an exhaust fan or near flammable items), pour into frying pan, and shake pan until flames die. Add tarragon, mustard, and half-and-half. Cook, stirring, until bubbly and thickened. Remove from heat, stir in lemon juice, and pour over veal and asparagus.

makes 6 servings

per serving: 305 calories, 27 g protein, 8 g carbohydrates, 19 g total fat, 126 mg cholesterol, 187 mg sodium

veal chops milanese

preparation time: about 30 minutes

6 boneless veal chops (about 1½ lbs. *total*),
   each ¾ to 1 inch thick

3 eggs

About 1 cup seasoned fine dry bread crumbs

About ⅓ cup all-purpose flour

Salt and pepper

About ¼ cup butter or margarine

About ¼ cup salad oil

Lemon wedges

1 Slash connective tissue around edge of each chop at 1-inch intervals, cutting just to meat. Then place chops between sheets of plastic wrap and pound with a flat-surfaced mallet until about ¼ inch thick. Set aside.

2 In a shallow pan, beat eggs to blend; spread crumbs in another shallow pan. Dredge chops in flour; shake off excess. Season to taste with salt and pepper. Dip each chop in eggs, drain briefly, and roll in crumbs to coat well, pressing crumbs into meat so they adhere. Set chops aside.

3 Melt 1 tablespoon of the butter in 1 tablespoon of the oil in a wide frying pan over medium-high heat. Add chops, a few at a time (do not crowd pan). Cook, turning once, until golden brown on both sides and just slightly pink in center; cut to test (about 4 minutes). Add more butter and oil to pan as needed. To serve, offer lemon wedges to squeeze over individual portions.

makes 6 servings

per serving: 467 calories, 28 g protein, 19 g carbohydrates, 30 g total fat, 218 mg cholesterol, 736 mg sodium

veal with mushrooms

preparation time: about 35 minutes

**1 pound veal scaloppine,
    cut into ¼- by 2-inch strips**

⅛ teaspoon salt

⅛ teaspoon pepper

8 ounces dried linguine

1 tablespoon butter or margarine

2 cloves garlic, minced or pressed

2 cups sliced mushrooms

½ cup marsala or cream sherry

3 tablespoons chopped parsley

1 large tomato, chopped and drained well

¼ cup pitted ripe olives, chopped

1 In a large bowl, mix veal, salt, and pepper; set aside.

2 In a 4- to 5-quart pan, cook linguine in about 8 cups boiling water until just tender to bite (8 to 10 minutes); or cook according to package directions. Drain well, transfer to a warm rimmed platter, and keep warm.

3 While pasta is cooking, melt butter in a wide nonstick frying pan or wok over medium-high heat. Add meat and garlic; stir-fry just until meat is no longer pink on outside (1 to 2 minutes). Add water, 1 tablespoon at a time, if pan appears dry. Remove meat from pan with a slotted spoon; keep warm.

4 Add mushrooms and 3 tablespoons water to pan. Stir-fry until mushrooms are soft (about 3 minutes), gently scraping any browned bits free from pan. Add marsala and bring to a boil; then boil, stirring, until sauce is slightly thickened (about 3 minutes). Remove pan from heat and stir in meat and parsley.

5 To serve, spoon meat mixture over pasta; sprinkle with chopped tomato and olives.

makes 4 servings

per serving: 440 calories, 33 g protein, 52 g carbohydrates, 7 g total fat, 96 mg cholesterol, 191 mg sodium

grilled veal chops
& vegetables

preparation time: about 15 minutes

1 tablespoon lemon juice

2 tablespoons olive oil or salad oil

¼ teaspoon dry marjoram

1 clove garlic, minced or pressed

1 small Japanese-type eggplant, unpeeled

**2 veal loin chops, about 1 inch thick
    (about 1 lb. *total*)**

**4 green onions (including tops) or baby leeks,
    ends trimmed**

Lemon zest

Salt and freshly ground pepper

1 Blend lemon juice, olive oil, marjoram, and garlic. Cut eggplant in half lengthwise. Brush veal chops, eggplant, and onions generously with oil mixture.

2 Place a ridged cooktop grill pan over medium-high heat and preheat until a drop of water dances on surface. Place chops in center of pan; add eggplant, cut sides down, and onions around chops. Cook, turning each ingredient once, until onions are tender-crisp (4 to 5 minutes total), chops are well browned on both sides and barely pink inside when cut near bone (6 to 8 minutes total), and eggplant is tender (about 8 minutes total).

3 Arrange veal and vegetables on warm dinner plates. Sprinkle each serving with lemon zest and season with salt and pepper to taste.

makes 2 servings

per serving: 456 calories, 37g protein, 5 g carbohydrates, 32 g total fat, 136 mg cholesterol, 92 mg sodium

barbecued lamb with blackberry sauce

preparation time: 20 minutes

½ cup seedless blackberry jam

⅓ cup balsamic or red wine vinegar

1 tablespoon Dijon mustard

1 tablespoon minced fresh rosemary
   or crumbled dried rosemary

1½ pounds lean boneless lamb (leg or loin),
   trimmed of fat and cut into 1-inch cubes

Salt

1 In a large bowl, stir together jam, vinegar, mustard, and rosemary. Pour a third of the jam mixture into a small container and set aside.

2 Add lamb cubes to remaining jam mixture in bowl; stir to coat well. Then thread lamb equally on four to six 12- to 14-inch metal skewers; discard marinade.

3 Place skewers on a lightly oiled grill 4 to 6 inches above a solid bed of medium-hot coals (you can hold your hand at grill level for 3 to 4 seconds) or over medium-high heat on a gas grill. Close lid on gas grill. Cook, turning as needed to brown evenly and basting with reserved jam mixture, until lamb is done to your liking; cut to test (about 7 minutes for medium-rare).

4 To serve, push lamb from skewers onto plates. Season to taste with salt.

makes 4 servings

per serving: 316 calories, 36 g protein, 18 g carbohydrates, 10 g total fat, 114 mg cholesterol, 159 mg sodium

lamb pilaf

preparation time: 30 minutes

1 pound lean ground lamb

1 large onion, chopped

1 package (6 to 8 oz.) rice pilaf mix
   with Middle Eastern seasonings

1 cucumber

1 cup plain nonfat yogurt

½ cup chopped parsley

2 tablespoons thinly sliced green onion

2 tablespoons chopped fresh mint

1 tablespoon lemon juice

Salt

Mint sprigs (optional)

1 Crumble lamb into a wide nonstick frying pan or 5- to 6-quart pan; add chopped onion. Cook over high heat, stirring often, until lamb is browned and onion is soft (about 6 minutes).

2 Spoon off and discard any fat from pan. Return pan to heat; add ¼ cup water and stir to scrape browned bits free. Then add pilaf mix (including seasoning packet) and amount of water specified in package directions for making entire mix. Bring to a boil; reduce heat, cover, and simmer until rice is tender to bite and liquid has been absorbed (about 15 minutes).

3 Meanwhile, coarsely chop cucumber. In a bowl, stir together yogurt, parsley, green onion, chopped mint, and lemon juice; add cucumber and mix gently. Season to taste with salt. Garnish with mint sprigs, if desired.

4 Transfer pilaf to a platter; serve with cucumber salad.

makes 6 servings

per serving: 293 calories, 19 g protein, 30 g carbohydrates, 11 g total fat, 51 mg cholesterol, 493 mg sodium

lemon bacon and red onions with calf's liver

preparation time: 45 minutes

8 slices (about ⅔ lb.) thick-cut bacon

¼ cup firmly packed brown sugar

1½ teaspoons grated lemon peel

½ to ¾ pound calf's liver,
   cut into ½-inch-thick slices

2 red onions, peeled and thinly sliced

3 tablespoons lemon juice

2 tablespoons butter or olive oil

1 cup minced parsley

About ¼ cup all-purpose flour

Salt and pepper

1 In a 10- by 15-inch rimmed pan, lay bacon slices side by side.

2 Bake in a 350° oven for 15 minutes. Drain and save fat.

3 Mix sugar and lemon peel. With your fingers, evenly pat mixture onto bacon slices, covering completely. Return pan to oven and bake until bacon is well browned, 12 to 15 minutes. With a wide spatula, transfer bacon to a rack; scrape sugar drippings from pan and put on bacon.

4 Meanwhile, rinse liver, pat dry, and trim off and discard any tough membrane. Cut liver into 4 equal portions.

5 In a 10- to 12-inch nonstick frying pan, combine onions, lemon juice, and butter. Stir over high heat until onions are limp and slightly browned, about 15 minutes. Add parsley and stir until wilted. Mound onions on an ovenproof platter; arrange bacon in a single layer alongside. Put in a 150° oven. Wipe frying pan clean.

6 Set frying pan over high heat and add reserved bacon fat. Coat liver with flour, shaking off excess. When fat is hot, add liver. Brown on each side, turning as needed until just barely pink in center (cut to test), about 5 minutes total. Drain liver briefly on towels, then add to platter. Add salt and pepper to taste.

makes 4 servings

per serving: 394 calories, 20 g protein, 21 g total fat, 33 g carbohydrates, 469 mg sodium, 210 mg cholesterol

pan-browned ham with braised fennel

preparation time: 25 minutes

2 heads fennel (*each* about 4 inches in diameter)

½ cup dry white wine or fat-free reduced-sodium chicken broth

1 pound thinly sliced cooked ham

Pepper

1 Rinse fennel. Cut off coarse stalks, reserving green leaves. Trim and discard base and any discolored or bruised parts from each fennel head. Slice fennel paper-thin, using a mandoline or a food processor. Chop reserved fennel leaves and set aside.

2 In a wide frying pan, combine sliced fennel and wine. Cook over high heat, stirring, until all but 1 to 2 tablespoons of the liquid have evaporated (about 5 minutes). Transfer fennel to a platter and keep warm.

3 Add as many ham slices to pan as will fit without crowding (you may need to cook ham in batches). Cook, stirring, until lightly browned (2 to 3 minutes). Arrange ham next to fennel.

4 Sprinkle chopped fennel leaves over ham and fennel. Season to taste with pepper.

makes 4 servings

per serving: 248 calories, 28 g protein, 5 g carbohydrates, 10 g total fat, 67 mg cholesterol, 1,857 mg sodium

butterflied sausages with barley-mushroom pilaf

preparation time: 25 minutes

1 tablespoon butter or margarine

1 large onion, chopped

1½ cups sliced mushrooms

1 cup quick-cooking barley

2 cups beef broth

¼ teaspoon dried thyme

¼ teaspoon dried marjoram

4 raw Italian sausages (¾ to 1 lb. *total*)

Chopped parsley

PLAN AHEAD FOR LEFTOVERS When time permits, cook a larger cut of meat—one that will yield more than enough for one meal. Roast beef, lamb, or veal can be sliced and quickly reheated; or use the meat in hot or cold sandwiches, stir-fries, or other dishes.

1 Melt butter in a wide nonstick frying pan over high heat. Add onion and mushrooms; cook, stirring often, until tinged with brown (about 3 minutes). Stir in barley, broth, thyme, and marjoram. Bring to a boil; then reduce heat, cover, and simmer until barley is tender to bite (10 to 12 minutes). Remove from heat and let stand, covered, until all liquid has been absorbed.

2 Meanwhile, make a half lengthwise cut in each sausage, cutting to within about ¼ inch of bottom surface. Gently press sausages open; then place, cut side up, in a foil-lined broiler pan.

3 Broil sausages 4 to 6 inches below heat, turning once, until evenly browned on both sides and cooked through; cut to test (8 to 10 minutes).

4 Spoon barley-mushroom pilaf into a wide bowl. Top with sausages and sprinkle with parsley.

makes 4 servings

per serving: 429 calories, 21 g protein, 35 g carbohydrates, 23 g total fat, 65 mg cholesterol, 1,115 mg sodium

sausages with grapes

preparation time: 30 minutes

4 mild Italian sausages (about 1 lb. *total*)

3 cups seedless green grapes

1 Prick sausages with a fork and place in a wide frying pan. Add 1 cup water. Bring to a boil over high heat; then reduce heat, cover, and simmer for 10 minutes.

2 Drain water and fat from pan. Add 2 cups of the grapes to pan; cover and simmer until grapes are soft (about 7 minutes). Uncover, increase heat to high, and continue to cook, turning sausages and stirring grapes occasionally. As liquid cooks away, reduce heat to medium; stir often until sausages are well browned and grapes are lightly browned (about 10 minutes). Stir in remaining 1 cup grapes.

3 Transfer sausages to a platter and spoon grapes over them.

makes 4 servings

per serving: 338 calories, 17 g protein, 19 g carbohydrates, 22 g total fat, 65 mg cholesterol, 767 mg sodium

pork tenderloins with stilton & port

preparation time: about 25 minutes

1 tablespoon salad oil

2 or 3 pork tenderloins (1½ lbs. *total*), trimmed of fat

1 cup port

½ cup regular-strength chicken broth

½ cup whipping cream

¼ pound Stilton cheese, crumbled

1 or 2 fresh jalapeño chiles, halved lengthwise, stemmed, seeded, and diced (optional)

1 Heat oil in a wide frying pan over medium-high heat. Add pork and cook, turning, until browned (about 4 minutes total). Transfer meat to a baking pan and bake in a 400° oven until a meat thermometer inserted in thickest part registers 160° (about 15 minutes).

2 Meanwhile, discard fat from frying pan and add port and broth. Boil over high heat until reduced to about ¼ cup (about 3 minutes). Stir in cream and continue to boil, stirring, until large, shiny bubbles form (about 5 more minutes). Add cheese and stir until melted; stir in jalapeños, if desired. Remove from heat.

3 Slice meat thinly across grain. Fan slices on warm plates and spoon sauce over meat.

makes 4 to 6 servings

per serving: 294 calories, 29 g protein, 6 g carbohydrates, 17 g total fat, 110 mg cholesterol, 414 mg sodium

gingered pork with asian pears

preparation time: about 35 minutes

3 large firm-ripe Asian or regular pears, peeled, cored, and thinly sliced

3 tablespoons cider vinegar

1 teaspoon vegetable oil

1 pound pork tenderloin, trimmed of fat and cut into 1-inch chunks

2 tablespoons firmly packed brown sugar

⅔ cup dry white wine

⅔ cup fat-free reduced-sodium chicken broth

2 teaspoons minced fresh ginger

4 teaspoons cornstarch blended with 4 teaspoons cold water

½ to ¾ cup finely shredded spinach

1 In a large bowl, gently mix pears and 1 tablespoon of the vinegar. Set aside.

2 Heat oil in a wide nonstick frying pan or wok over medium-high heat. When oil is hot, add pork and stir-fry until lightly browned on outside and no longer pink in center; cut to test (about 8 minutes). Add water, 1 tablespoon at a time, if pan appears dry. Remove meat from pan with a slotted spoon; keep warm.

3 Add sugar and remaining 2 tablespoons vinegar to pan. Bring to a boil; then boil, stirring, for 1 minute. Add wine, broth, and ginger; return to a boil. Boil, stirring, for 3 minutes. Add pears and cook, gently turning pears often, until pears are heated through (about 3 minutes). Stir cornstarch mixture well and pour into pan. Cook, stirring, until sauce boils and thickens slightly (1 to 2 minutes).

4 Remove pan from heat; return meat to pan and mix gently but thoroughly. Gently stir in spinach.

makes 4 servings

per serving: 309 calories, 25 g protein, 34 g carbohydrates, 6 g total fat, 74 mg cholesterol, 177 mg sodium

pork medallions with prunes

preparation time: about 40 minutes

1 pork tenderloin (about ¾ lb.), trimmed of fat
   and cut across the grain into 1-inch-thick slices

¾ cup Madeira

½ cup regular-strength beef broth

1 tablespoon red wine vinegar

2 teaspoons cornstarch

3 whole cloves

2 tablespoons butter or margarine

12 moist-pack pitted prunes

⅓ cup chopped shallots

Watercress sprigs

Salt

1 Place pork slices between sheets of plastic wrap and pound with a flat-surfaced mallet until about ⅜ inch thick. In a small bowl, stir together Madeira, broth, vinegar, cornstarch, and cloves; set aside.

2 Melt butter in a wide frying pan over medium-high heat. Add pork, a portion at a time (do not crowd pan). Cook, turning once, until well browned on both sides and no longer pink in center; cut to test (4 to 5 minutes). As pork is cooked, transfer to a warm plate and keep warm.

3 After all pork is done, add prunes to pan, turning them in drippings to warm; then lift from pan with a slotted spoon and place on plate with pork. Add shallots to pan and cook, stirring, until limp. Add Madeira mixture and any accumulated pork juices; bring to a boil, stirring.

4 To serve, arrange pork and prunes on 3 warm dinner plates; spoon sauce over meat and fruit. Garnish with watercress and season to taste with salt.

makes 3 servings

per serving: 327 calories, 26 g protein, 33 g carbohydrates, 11 g total fat, 94 mg cholesterol, 280 mg sodium

baked pork chops dijon

preparation time: about 30 minutes

6 loin pork chops (about 2½ lbs. *total*),
   each about ¾ inch thick

6 tablespoons olive oil or salad oil

¼ cup red wine vinegar

2 tablespoons Dijon mustard

1 tablespoon minced chives

1 teaspoon dry tarragon

Freshly ground pepper

1 Arrange chops in a foil-lined rimmed baking pan. In a small bowl, whisk together oil, vinegar, mustard, chives, and tarragon; season to taste with pepper. Spread 1 tablespoon of the mustard baste over each chop.

2 Bake on upper rack of a 475° oven for 10 minutes. Turn chops over and spread each one with 1 more tablespoon of the baste. Continue to bake until meat in thickest part is no longer pink; cut to test (8 to 10 more minutes).

makes 6 servings

per serving: 401 calories, 28 g protein, 1 g carbohydrates, 31 g total fat, 101 mg cholesterol, 146 mg sodium

pork tenderloin with bulgur

preparation time: about 40 minutes

3 cups beef broth

1 cup bulgur (cracked wheat)

½ cup sliced green onions

1½ pounds pork tenderloin (about 2 tenderloins), trimmed of fat

2 teaspoons sugar

1 tablespoon vegetable oil

1 tablespoon mustard seeds

1 tablespoon balsamic vinegar

2 teaspoons minced fresh oregano or 1 teaspoon dried oregano

½ cup dry red wine

2 teaspoons cornstarch mixed with 2 teaspoons cold water

1 pound asparagus, tough ends broken off

Salt and pepper

1 In a 2- to 3-quart pan, bring 2 cups of the broth to a boil; stir in bulgur. Cover, remove from heat, and let stand until bulgur is tender to bite (about 30 minutes). Stir in onions.

2 While bulgur is standing, sprinkle pork with sugar. Heat oil in a wide frying pan over medium-high heat; add pork and cook, turning as needed, until browned on all sides (about 4 minutes). Add ⅔ cup of the broth, mustard seeds, vinegar, and oregano. Cover, reduce heat to medium-low, and simmer just until meat is no longer pink in center; cut to test (about 12 minutes).

3 Lift pork to a warm platter and keep warm. To pan, add wine and remaining ⅓ cup broth. Bring to a boil over high heat; then boil until reduced to ¾ cup (about 2 minutes). Stir in cornstarch mixture; return to a boil, stirring.

4 While sauce is boiling, bring ½ inch of water to a boil in another wide frying pan over high heat. Add asparagus and cook, uncovered, just until barely tender when pierced (about 4 minutes). Drain. Slice pork; mound bulgur alongside, then top with asparagus. Spoon sauce over meat. Season to taste with salt and pepper.

makes 4 servings

per serving: 442 calories, 45 g protein, 36 g carbohydrates, 11 g total fat, 111 mg cholesterol, 1,327 mg sodium

stir-fried pork with green onions

preparation time: about 15 minute

½ pound boneless pork, such as loin or shoulder

1 tablespoon cornstarch

1 tablespoon rice wine or dry sherry

2 tablespoons salad oil

½ pound green onions (including tops), cut into slivers

3 cloves garlic, minced or pressed

Salt and pepper

1 Cut pork across the grain into thin slices; then cut each slice into matchstick-size strips. In a bowl, combine cornstarch and wine; add pork and stir to coat well.

2 Heat oil in a wok or wide frying pan over high heat. Add pork mixture and cook, stirring, until lightly browned (2 to 3 minutes). Add onions and garlic and continue to cook, stirring, until heated through (2 to 3 more minutes). Season to taste with salt and pepper.

makes 2 servings

per serving: 486 calories, 23 g protein, 12 g carbohydrates, 38 g total fat, 79 mg cholesterol, 70 mg sodium

lamb curry

preparation time: 25 minutes

1 pound lean ground lamb

1 large onion, chopped

2 teaspoons cornstarch

1 can (about 14½ oz.) beef broth

2 cloves garlic, minced or pressed

1 tablespoon curry powder

½ teaspoon ground ginger

½ teaspoon ground cumin

1 large carrot, thinly sliced

1 large apple, peeled, cored, and chopped

1 large green bell pepper, seeded and chopped

Salt and ground red pepper (cayenne)

Chutney

Plain yogurt

1 Crumble lamb into a wide nonstick frying pan; add onion. Cook over high heat, stirring often, until lamb and onion are browned (about 6 minutes). Meanwhile, in a small bowl, stir together cornstarch and 2 tablespoons of the broth; set aside.

2 Spoon off and discard any fat from pan. Reduce heat to medium-low. Add garlic, curry powder, ginger, cumin, carrot, apple, bell pepper, and remaining broth. Bring to a simmer; then simmer, uncovered, until all vegetables are tender to bite (about 12 minutes).

3 Stir in cornstarch mixture; simmer, stirring often, until sauce is thickened. Season to taste with salt and red pepper. Offer chutney and yogurt to add to taste.

makes 4 servings

per serving: 318 calories, 22 g protein, 21 g carbohydrates, 16 g total fat, 76 mg cholesterol, 436 mg sodium

butterflied leg of lamb with herbs & feta

preparation time: 25 minutes

1 boneless butterflied leg of lamb (4 to 4½ lbs.), trimmed of fat

2 cloves garlic, thinly sliced

1 tablespoon minced fresh rosemary or crumbled dried rosemary

5 tablespoons minced fresh basil

½ cup crumbled feta cheese

Salt and pepper

1 Lay lamb flat, boned side up. Cut slits about ½ inch deep all over lamb. Fit garlic slices into slits. Rub rosemary and 1 tablespoon of the basil over both sides of lamb.

2 Thread 2 long (at least 18-inch) metal skewers parallel to each other lengthwise through lamb. Then place lamb on a lightly oiled grill 4 to 6 inches above a solid bed of very hot coals (you can hold your hand at grill level for only 1 to 2 seconds) or over very high heat on a gas grill. Close lid on gas grill. Cook, turning as needed to brown evenly, until a meat thermometer inserted in thickest part of lamb (not touching skewer) registers 140° F for medium-rare (about 17 minutes). Or cut meat to test. Thinner parts will be more done.

3 Transfer lamb to a carving board; sprinkle with cheese and remaining ¼ cup basil. Remove skewers and slice lamb. Season to taste with salt and pepper.

makes about 16 servings

per serving: 185 calories, 26 g protein, 0 g carbohydrates, 8 g total fat, 84 mg cholesterol, 109 mg sodium

butterflied pork loin with apricot-sesame glaze

preparation time: 25 minutes

⅓ cup apricot jam

2 tablespoons seasoned rice vinegar

1 tablespoon Asian sesame oil

1 boneless center-cut pork loin roast
   (2½ to 3 lbs.), trimmed of fat

6 to 8 green onions, ends trimmed

2 teaspoons sesame seeds

Salt

1 In a small bowl, stir together jam, vinegar, and oil; set aside.

2 Make a lengthwise cut down center of pork, cutting to within 1 inch of bottom surface; then press pork open to make a butterfly shape. Make a similar lengthwise cut through each of the 2 thick sections. Pull cuts open; press pork to make it 1¼ to 1½ inches thick. (If necessary, cut pork lengthwise again and pull these cuts open.)

3 Thread 2 long (at least 18-inch) metal skewers parallel to each other lengthwise through pork. Then place pork on a lightly oiled grill above a solid bed of very hot coals (you can hold your hand at grill level for only 1 to 2 seconds) or over very high heat on a gas grill. Brush pork with half the jam mixture. Close lid on gas grill. Cook, turning as needed to brown evenly, until meat in thickest part is no longer pink; cut to test (about 18 minutes). Near end of cooking time, grill onions, turning once, until lightly browned; remove onions from grill as they are done. Just before pork is done, brush it with remaining jam mixture and sprinkle evenly with sesame seeds.

4 Transfer pork to a carving board. Remove skewers and slice meat thinly. Accompany with grilled green onions; season to taste with salt.

makes 10 to 12 servings

per serving: 221 calories, 25 g protein, 8 g carbohydrates, 10 g total fat, 67 mg cholesterol, 114 mg sodium

thai-spiced loin chops with hot-sweet mustard

preparation time: 10 minutes

About 1¼ teaspoons Thai red curry paste

4 boneless center-cut pork loin chops
   (about 1¼ lbs. *total*), *each* about ½ inch
   thick, trimmed of fat

Cilantro sprigs

½ cup prepared hot-sweet mustard

1 Spread about ⅛ teaspoon of the curry paste on each side of each chop. Place chops on a lightly oiled grill 4 to 6 inches above a solid bed of hot coals (you can hold your hand at grill level for only 2 to 3 seconds) or over high heat on a gas grill. Close lid on gas grill. Cook, turning once, until pork is still moist and looks faintly pink to white in center; cut to test (5 to 7 minutes).

2 Garnish chops with cilantro sprigs. Offer mustard to add to taste.

makes 4 servings

per serving: 267 calories, 31 g protein, 12 g carbohydrates, 8 g total fat, 90 mg cholesterol, 140 mg sodium

pork with garlic & green onions

preparation time: 20 minutes

8 ounces boneless pork (such as loin, shoulder, or butt), trimmed of fat

1 tablespoon cornstarch

1 tablespoon rice wine or dry sherry

6 green onions

1 teaspoon vegetable oil

1 tablespoon minced garlic

2 teaspoons soy sauce

1 Cut pork into matchstick strips. In a large bowl, mix pork, cornstarch, and wine.

2 Cut onions crosswise into 1-inch pieces; then cut each onion piece lengthwise into thin slivers.

3 Heat a wide nonstick frying pan over high heat. Add oil and swirl to coat pan bottom. Add pork mixture and cook, stirring, until meat is lightly browned (2 to 3 minutes). Add onions and garlic; cook, stirring, until onions are slightly softer and garlic is tinged with brown (1 to 2 minutes). Stir in soy sauce.

makes 2 servings

per serving: 232 calories, 26 g protein, 9 g carbohydrates, 9 g total fat, 67 mg cholesterol, 412 mg sodium

sweet & sour pork

preparation time: about 40 minutes

⅓ cup plus 4 teaspoons cornstarch

¼ cup white wine vinegar or distilled white vinegar

¼ cup sugar

1 tablespoon catsup

1 tablespoon reduced-sodium soy sauce

⅛ teaspoon hot chili oil, or to taste

1 large egg white

1 pound pork tenderloin, trimmed of fat and cut into 1-inch chunks

1 tablespoon vegetable oil

1 large onion, cut into thin wedges

1 large green bell pepper, seeded and cut into 1-inch squares

1 or 2 cloves garlic, minced or pressed

1 large tomato, cut into wedges

1½ cups fresh or canned pineapple chunks, drained

1 For sweet-sour sauce, in a medium-size bowl, stir together 4 teaspoons of the cornstarch and the vinegar until blended. Stir in ¾ cup water, sugar, catsup, soy sauce and hot chile oil. Set aside.

2 In a medium-size bowl, beat egg white to blend well. Place remaining ⅓ cup cornstarch in another medium-size bowl. Dip pork chunks, a portion at a time, in egg white; then coat lightly with cornstarch and shake off excess.

3 Heat vegetable oil in a wide nonstick frying pan or wok over medium-high heat. When oil is hot, add meat and stir-fry gently until golden brown on outside and no longer pink in center; cut to test (about 8 minutes). Add water, 1 tablespoon at a time, if pan appears dry. Remove meat from pan with a slotted spoon; keep warm.

4 Add onion, bell pepper, garlic, and 1 tablespoon water to pan; stir-fry for 1 minute. Add more water, 1 tablespoon at a time, if pan appears dry. Stir reserved sweet-sour sauce well and pour into pan. Cook, stirring, until sauce boils and thickens slightly (2 to 3 minutes).

5 Add tomato, pineapple, and meat to pan. Cook, stirring gently but thoroughly, just until heated through (1 to 2 minutes). Serve immediately.

makes 4 servings

per serving: 355 calories, 27 g protein, 45 g carbohydrates, 8 g total fat, 74 mg cholesterol, 275 mg sodium

sautéed lamb with apples

preparation time: about 30 minutes

4 to 8 large radicchio leaves, rinsed and crisped

1 pound lean boneless leg of lamb, trimmed of fat and cut into ³⁄₄-inch chunks

¼ teaspoon salt

⅛ teaspoon pepper

⅓ cup apple jelly

⅓ cup cider vinegar

1 tablespoon cornstarch blended with 1 tablespoon cold water

1 teaspoon Dijon mustard

³⁄₄ teaspoon chopped fresh thyme or ¼ teaspoon dried thyme

⅓ cup dried currants or raisins

3 large Golden Delicious apples, peeled, cored, and sliced ½ inch thick

2 teaspoons vegetable oil

1 to 2 tablespoons chopped parsley

Thyme sprigs

1 Arrange 1 or 2 radicchio leaves on each of 4 individual plates; cover and set aside.

2 In a large bowl, mix lamb, salt, and pepper; set aside. In a small bowl, stir together jelly, 3 tablespoons of the vinegar, cornstarch mixture, mustard, and chopped thyme until well blended. Stir in currants and set aside. In a medium-size bowl, gently mix apples with remaining vinegar.

3 Heat 1 teaspoon of the oil in a wide nonstick frying pan or wok over medium-high heat. When oil is hot, add apples and stir-fry gently until almost tender when pierced (about 4 minutes). Add water, 1 tablespoon at a time, if pan appears dry. Stir jelly mixture well; pour into pan and cook, stirring, just until sauce boils and thickens slightly (1 to 2 minutes). Remove apple mixture from pan and keep warm. Wipe pan clean.

4 Heat remaining 1 teaspoon oil in pan over medium-high heat. When oil is hot, add meat and stir-fry just until done to your liking; cut to test (about 3 minutes for medium-rare). Remove from heat and stir in parsley.

5 Spoon meat into radicchio leaves; spoon apple mixture alongside. Garnish with thyme sprigs.

makes 4 servings

per serving: 367 calories, 25 g protein, 52 g carbohydrates, 8 g total fat, 73 mg cholesterol, 114 mg sodium

broiled lamb chops with cherry sauce

preparation time: 25 minutes

2 tablespoons orange juice

1 teaspoon cornstarch

⅓ cup currant jelly

¼ cup balsamic vinegar

½ teaspoon dried tarragon

³⁄₄ cup canned pitted dark sweet cherries, drained

8 lamb rib chops (about 1³⁄₄ lbs. *total*), trimmed of fat, bones Frenched

1 In a small bowl, stir together orange juice and cornstarch. Set aside.

2 In a 1½- to 2-quart pan, combine jelly, vinegar, and tarragon. Stir over high heat until steaming. Stir in orange juice mixture and bring to a simmer; mixture will thicken slightly. Stir in cherries; then remove from heat and keep warm.

3 Arrange lamb chops on a rack in a broiler pan. Broil 4 to 6 inches below heat, turning once, until lightly browned on both sides and done to your liking; cut to test (10 to 12 minutes for medium-rare).

4 Transfer lamb chops to a platter and top with cherry sauce.

makes 4 servings

per serving: 245 calories, 18 g protein, 24 g carbohydrates, 9 g total fat, 58 mg cholesterol, 64 mg sodium

pounded lamb chops with rosemary

preparation time: about 20 minutes

4 lamb rib or loin chops (about 1¼ lbs. *total*), each ¾ to 1 inch thick

4 cloves garlic, minced or pressed

2 tablespoons minced fresh rosemary or 1 tablespoon dry rosemary

½ cup minced parsley

2 tablespoons olive oil or salad oil

Rosemary sprigs (optional)

1 Slash fat around edge of each lamb chop at 1-inch intervals, cutting just to meat. Stir together garlic, minced rosemary, parsley, and oil. Rub each side of each chop with about 1 tablespoon of the rosemary mixture, then place chops between sheets of plastic wrap and pound with a flat-surfaced mallet until meat is about ¼ inch thick.

2 Place chops on a greased grill about 6 inches above a solid bed of hot coals. Cook, turning once, until done to your liking; cut to test (about 4 minutes for medium-rare). Garnish with rosemary sprigs, if desired.

makes 4 servings

per serving: 288 calories, 31 g protein, 2 g carbohydrates, 17 g total fat, 96 mg cholesterol, 89 mg sodium

lamb shish kebabs

preparation time: about 55 minutes

1 to 1½ pounds lean boneless lamb (shoulder or leg), cut into 1½-inch cubes

Lemon Marinade (recipe follows)

1 medium-size red or green bell pepper

1 medium-size white onion

8 medium-size mushrooms

1 Trim and discard excess fat from lamb; place lamb in a bowl. Prepare Lemon Marinade and pour over lamb; let marinate for 15 to 20 minutes. Seed bell pepper and cut into 1½-inch squares; cut onion into 8 wedges and separate each into layers.

2 Remove lamb from marinade and drain briefly; reserve marinade. Divide lamb into 4 equal portions; thread lamb and vegetables alternately on four 10- to 12-inch metal skewers, starting and ending each skewer with a mushroom. Place skewers on greased rack of a broiler pan. Pour marinade into a small pan and bring to a boil over high heat.

3 Broil lamb 3 to 4 inches below heat, turning as needed and basting frequently with marinade, until browned on all sides but still pink in center; cut to test (10 to 15 minutes).

LEMON MARINADE

Mix 2 tablespoons chopped parsley, ⅓ cup salad oil, 1 tablespoon soy sauce, ½ teaspoon *each* dry mustard and Worcestershire, ¼ cup lemon juice, and 1 clove garlic (minced or pressed).

makes 4 servings

per serving: 305 calories, 31 g protein, 5 g carbohydrates, 17 g total fat, 96 mg cholesterol, 219 mg sodium

grilled lamb chops with romesco sauce

preparation time: about 40 minutes

2 tablespoons slivered almonds

2 tablespoons olive oil

1 onion, peeled and chopped

2 cloves garlic, peeled and minced or pressed

1 ripe tomato, rinsed, cored, and chopped

¾ cup chopped canned red peppers

¼ to ½ teaspoon hot chili flakes

3 tablespoons red wine vinegar

Salt and pepper

12 lamb rib chops (*each* about ¾ in. thick and 3 to 4 oz.)

1 In a 10- to 12-inch frying pan over medium heat, stir almonds until golden, about 5 minutes. Whirl nuts in a food processor or blender until finely ground.

2 Add oil, onion, and garlic to pan; stir over high heat until onion is limp, about 3 minutes. Add tomato, red peppers, chili flakes, and vinegar. Simmer over medium heat, stirring occasionally, until most of the liquid is evaporated, 6 to 8 minutes.

3 Stir ground almonds into tomato mixture; add salt and pepper to taste. Pour romesco sauce into a bowl.

4 Rinse lamb and pat dry. Trim and discard excess surface fat. Lay chops on a barbecue grill over a solid bed of hot coals or high heat on a gas grill (you can hold your hand at grill level only 2 to 3 seconds); close lid on gas grill. Cook, turning once until browned on both sides but still pink in center of thickest part (cut to test), 8 to 10 minutes total. Add salt and pepper to taste.

5 Serve with hot or cool romesco sauce.

per serving: 106 calories, 8.1 g protein, 3.5 g carbohydrates, 6.6 g total fat, 25 mg cholesterol, 42 mg sodium

baked lamb meatballs with pine nuts

preparation time: 25 minutes

1 egg

½ teaspoon *each* salt and ground cinnamon

1 clove garlic, minced or pressed

2 tablespoons *each* fine dry bread crumbs and catsup

1 tablespoon red wine vinegar

¼ cup pine nuts or slivered almonds

1½ pounds lean ground lamb

1 tablespoon olive oil

1 small red onion, thinly sliced

½ cup Marsala or cream sherry

2 teaspoons lemon juice

Chopped parsley

1 Beat egg until blended; mix in salt, cinnamon, garlic, bread crumbs, catsup, and vinegar. Add pine nuts and lamb; mix lightly. Shape mixture into 1½-inch meatballs. Set slightly apart in a shallow rimmed baking pan. Bake in a 500° oven until well browned (10 to 12 minutes).

2 Meanwhile, heat oil in a medium-size frying pan over medium heat. Add onion and cook, stirring often, until soft and lightly browned (6 to 8 minutes). Remove pan from heat and set aside.

3 With a slotted spoon, transfer meatballs to a warm serving dish and keep warm. Pour off and discard fat from baking pan. Pour a little of the wine into baking pan, scraping browned bits free; add to onion mixture along with remaining wine and lemon juice. Boil over high heat, stirring, until liquid is reduced by about half. Pour over meatballs and sprinkle with parsley.

makes 4 servings

per serving: 537 calories, 30 g protein, 10 g carbohydrates, 42 g total fat, 186 mg cholesterol, 468 mg sodium

simple sukiyaki

preparation time: 20 minutes

½ cup condensed consommé

¼ cup dry sherry

¼ cup reduced-sodium soy sauce

1 tablespoon sugar

4 ounces packaged triple-washed baby spinach

½ teaspoon vegetable oil

8 ounces lean boneless beef ribeye or sirloin, trimmed of fat and thinly sliced

1 tablespoon minced fresh ginger

1 medium-size onion, thinly sliced

1 cup sliced mushrooms

4 green onions, cut into 1-inch lengths

Hot cooked rice

1 In a small bowl, stir together consommé, sherry, soy sauce, and sugar. Set aside. Remove and discard any coarse stems from spinach; set spinach aside.

2 Heat oil in a wide nonstick frying pan over high heat. Add beef and ginger; cook, stirring, until beef is browned (2 to 3 minutes). With a slotted spoon, transfer beef and ginger to a bowl.

3 Add sliced onion and mushrooms to pan; cook, stirring, until onion is soft and mushrooms are tinged with brown (about 3 minutes). Add green onions and spinach; stir until spinach is wilted (about 1 minute). Add consommé mixture, then return beef to pan; bring to a boil, stirring. Serve over rice.

makes 2 servings

per serving: 353 calories, 31 g protein, 25 g carbohydrates, 11 g total fat, 67 mg cholesterol, 1,650 mg sodium

citrus beef stir-fry

preparation time: 25 minutes

2 large oranges

3 tablespoons dry sherry

3 tablespoons soy sauce

1 tablespoon cornstarch

1 pound lean boneless beef such as top sirloin, trimmed of fat and cut across the grain into ¼-inch-thick slices

2 tablespoons minced fresh ginger

1½ cups bean sprouts

1½ cups fresh Chinese pea pods, ends and strings removed

1 Grate peel (colored part only) from 1 orange. Squeeze juice from both oranges. Measure juice; if you have less than ¾ cup, add enough water to equal this amount. In a small bowl, stir together orange peel, orange juice, sherry, soy sauce, and cornstarch. Set aside.

2 Heat a wok or wide nonstick frying pan over high heat. When pan is hot, add beef and ginger. Cook, stirring, until beef is browned (2 to 3 minutes). With a slotted spoon, transfer beef to a bowl.

3 Pour orange juice mixture into pan and bring to a simmer. Add bean sprouts and pea pods; cook, stirring, until pea pods turn a brighter green (about 1 minute). Mix in beef and serve.

makes 4 servings

per serving: 243 calories, 28 g protein, 17 g carbohydrates, 5 g total fat, 69 mg cholesterol, 844 mg sodium

fajitas stir-fry

preparation time: about 35 minutes

8 flour tortillas (*each* 7 to 8 inches in diameter)

¼ cup salad oil

1 pound lean beef steak, such as sirloin
  or top round (about 1 inch thick), cut into
  ⅛-inch-thick strips

2 cloves garlic, minced or pressed

1 large onion, thinly sliced and separated
  into rings

2 or 3 fresh jalapeño chiles, stemmed, seeded,
  and minced

1 large red bell pepper, seeded and cut into
  thin strips

2 teaspoons ground cumin

3 tablespoons lime juice

1 teaspoon cornstarch

2 medium-size pear-shaped tomatoes, seeded
  and diced

Salt and pepper

1 large firm-ripe avocado

Lime wedges

Sour cream

1 Stack tortillas, wrap in foil, and place in a 350° oven until heated through (about 15 minutes).

2 Meanwhile, heat 1 tablespoon of the oil in a wok or wide frying pan over high heat. Add a third of the beef and cook, stirring, until lightly browned (about 2 minutes). With a slotted spoon, transfer beef to a bowl. Repeat to brown remaining beef, using 2 more tablespoons of the oil.

3 Add remaining 1 tablespoon oil to pan; then add garlic, onion, chiles, and bell pepper. Cook, stirring, until onion is tender-crisp to bite (about 2 minutes). In a small bowl, mix cumin, lime juice, and corn-starch; add to pan. Stir in tomatoes, then add beef and accumulated juices; bring to a boil, stirring. Season mixture to taste with salt and pepper, then transfer to a warm serving dish and keep warm.

4 Pit, peel, and dice avocado. Spoon beef mixture into warm tortillas; offer avocado, lime wedges, and sour cream to add to taste.

makes 4 servings

per serving: 647 calories, 34 g protein, 63 g carbohydrates, 29 g total fat, 69 mg cholesterol, 502 mg sodium

broiled steak with swiss mustard sauce

preparation time: about 20 minutes

1 Porterhouse steak (about 1½ inches thick)

3 tablespoons butter or margarine

1 tablespoon Dijon mustard

2 tablespoons dry vermouth or dry white wine

¼ teaspoon Worcestershire

1 Slash fat around edge of steak at 2- to 3-inch intervals, cutting just to lean meat. Place steak on lightly greased rack of a broiler pan. Broil 3 to 4 inches below heat, turning once, until done to your liking; cut to test (10 to 15 minutes for rare to medium-rare).

2 Meanwhile, melt butter in a small pan over medium-high heat. Blend in mustard, vermouth, and Worcestershire. Transfer steak to a warm platter; pour sauce around or over meat. Slice steak, swirling slices in sauce before transferring them to individual plates.

makes 3 servings

per serving: 593 calories, 39 g protein, 2 g carbohydrates, 47 g total fat, 162 mg cholesterol, 368 mg sodium

pepper beef stir-fry

preparation time: about 40 minutes

1 pound sirloin steak (about 1 inch thick),
    cut into ⅛-inch-thick strips

2 teaspoons cracked pepper

1 clove garlic, minced or pressed

2 tablespoons Worcestershire

¼ cup salad oil

1 large onion, thinly sliced

1 *each* large red and green bell pepper;
    seeded and cut into thin strips

Salt

1 In a bowl, mix beef, cracked pepper, garlic, and Worcestershire; set aside for 15 minutes.

2 Heat 1 tablespoon of the oil in a wok or wide frying pan over high heat. Add a third of the beef and cook, stirring, until lightly browned (about 2 minutes). With a slotted spoon, transfer beef to a bowl; keep warm. Repeat to brown remaining beef, using 2 more tablespoons of the oil.

3 Add remaining 1 tablespoon oil to pan, then add onion and bell peppers; cook, stirring, just until vegetables are tender-crisp to bite (about 2 minutes). Stir in beef and accumulated juices. Season to taste with salt.

makes 4 servings

per serving: 404 calories, 23 g protein, 8 g carbohydrates, 31 g total fat, 76 mg cholesterol, 146 mg sodium

smoked pork chops with ruote

preparation time: about 35 minutes

4 smoked pork loin chops, *each* about ¼ inch
    thick, trimmed of fat

8 ounces dried ruote or other medium-size pasta

1 tablespoon butter or margarine

1 large onion, chopped

1 tablespoon all-purpose flour

1 ½ cups nonfat milk

1 tablespoon Dijon mustard

¼ teaspoon pepper

1 package (about 10 oz.) frozen tiny peas

1 cup shredded Emmenthaler or Swiss cheese

1 Place pork chops in a wide nonstick frying pan and cook over medium-high heat, turning as needed, until browned on both sides (about 10 minutes). Transfer to a platter and keep warm. Discard any pan drippings.

2 Bring 8 cups water to a boil in a 4- to 5-quart pan over medium- high heat. Stir in pasta and cook just until tender to bite (8 to 10 minutes); or cook according to package directions. Meanwhile, melt butter in frying pan over medium-high heat. Add onion and cook, stirring often, until soft (about 5 minutes). Stir in flour and remove from heat. Add milk, mustard, and pepper; mix until blended.

3 Stir peas into pasta and water; drain and set aside. Return sauce to medium-high heat and cook, stirring, until mixture comes to a boil. Add cheese and stir until melted. Remove from heat and add pasta mixture. Mix thoroughly but gently. Spoon alongside pork chops.

makes 4 servings

per serving: 593 calories, 43 g protein, 63 g carbohydrates, 17 g total fat, 86 mg cholesterol, 1,867 mg sodium

broiled flank steak

preparation time: about 45 minutes

1 clove garlic, minced or pressed

⅓ cup salad oil

3 tablespoons red wine vinegar

2 teaspoons *each* Worcestershire, soy sauce, and dry mustard

¼ teaspoon pepper

Few drops of liquid hot pepper seasoning

1 to 1½ pounds flank steak, trimmed of fat

1 In a shallow dish, mix garlic, oil, vinegar, Worcestershire, soy sauce, mustard, pepper, and hot pepper seasoning. Place steak in dish; turn to coat with marinade. Let stand for 30 minutes, turning over several times.

2 Remove steak from marinade; drain briefly, reserving marinade. Place steak on lightly greased rack of a broiler pan. Pour marinade into a small pan and bring to a boil over high heat. Broil steak about 4 inches below heat, turning once and basting several times with marinade, until done to your liking; cut to test (8 to 10 minutes for rare).

3 To serve, cut steak across the grain into thin, slanting slices.

makes 4 to 6 servings

per serving: 323 calories, 22 g protein, 1 g carbohydrates, 25 g total fat, 56 mg cholesterol, 228 mg sodium

pan-browned spice steak

preparation time: about 40 minutes

¼ cup butter or margarine

4 medium-size sweet potatoes or yams, peeled and diced

1 tablespoon *each* juniper berries, whole black peppercorns, and whole allspice

1¼ to 1½ pounds flank steak or skirt steak, trimmed of fat and cut into 4 pieces

1 tablespoon salad oil

2 tablespoons gin or water

Watercress or parsley sprigs

Pickled onions

Salt

1 Place butter in a shallow 10- by 15-inch baking pan and heat in a 450° oven until melted. Add potatoes; stir to coat with butter. Return to oven and bake, turning potatoes several times with a wide spatula, until potatoes are lightly browned and soft when pressed with a fork (about 30 minutes).

2 Meanwhile, in a blender or food processor, whirl juniper berries, peppercorns, and allspice until coarsely ground. Press mixture into all sides of each piece of steak.

3 About 10 minutes before potatoes are done, heat oil in a wide frying pan over medium-high heat. Add steaks and cook, turning once, until well browned on both sides and rare in center; cut to test (3 to 5 minutes). Lift steaks from pan and keep warm. (To cook steaks further, place in oven with potatoes until meat is done to your liking.)

4 Add gin to pan, stirring to scrape browned bits free. Add potatoes; mix lightly to coat. Garnish steak and potatoes with watercress and pickled onions. Season to taste with salt.

makes 4 servings

per serving: 570 calories, 35 g protein, 42 g carbohydrates, 27 g total fat, 109 mg cholesterol, 255 mg sodium

lemon-mint lamb meatballs

preparation time: about 40 minutes

2 pounds lean ground lamb

2 eggs

¼ cup all-purpose flour

1 tablespoon dry mint

½ teaspoon *each* salt and pepper

2 tablespoons salad oil

⅓ cup finely chopped parsley

1¾ cups thinly sliced green onions
   (including tops)

Hot cooked rice

1 can (14½ oz.) regular-strength chicken broth

⅓ cup lemon juice

1 tablespoon *each* cornstarch and water

Lemon zest

Mint sprigs

1 In a large bowl, combine lamb, eggs, flour, dry mint, salt, and pepper; mix well, then shape into 1½-inch balls. Set slightly apart on an ungreased large rimmed baking sheet. Bake in a 500° oven until well browned (about 10 minutes).

2 Meanwhile, heat oil in a wide frying pan over medium heat; add parsley and 1½ cups of the onions and cook, stirring often, until onions are soft. Remove pan from heat.

3 With a slotted spoon, arrange meatballs over a bed of hot cooked rice in a serving dish; keep warm. Discard drippings from baking pan. Pour a small amount of the broth into pan and stir to scrape browned bits free; then pour broth mixture into frying pan and add remaining broth and lemon juice. Place pan over medium-high heat. In a small bowl, stir together cornstarch and water; stir into broth mixture and cook, stirring, until sauce is thickened. Pour sauce over meatballs and garnish with remaining ¼ cup onions, lemon zest, and mint sprigs.

makes 8 servings

per serving: 323 calories, 24 g protein, 6 g carbohydrates, 22 g total fat, 136 mg cholesterol, 449 mg sodium

lamb-stuffed celery

preparation time: about 35 minutes

1½ pounds ground lamb

4 cloves garlic, minced or pressed

2 eggs

¼ cup finely chopped fresh mint leaves
   or 1 tablespoon dry mint

Salt and pepper

8 to 10 large celery stalks

Prepared horseradish or mustard

1 With a fork, blend together lamb, garlic, eggs, and mint. Season to taste with salt and pepper. Set aside.

2 Cut leaves from celery and reserve for garnish (use leaves from inner stalks, if necessary). With a vegetable peeler, remove tough strings from celery. Rinse and pat dry.

3 Pack ⅓ to ½ cup of the meat mixture, mounding slightly, in hollow of each stalk. Arrange, meat sides up, slightly apart in a large baking pan. Bake in a 400° oven until meat is browned (about 25 minutes).

4 Arrange stalks on a warm serving platter with leaves at one end. Offer horseradish to add to each portion.

makes 4 or 5 servings

per serving: 399 calories, 26 g protein, 5 g carbohydrates, 30 g total fat, 210 mg cholesterol, 171 mg sodium

olive-crusted lamb chops

preparation time: about 30 minutes

4 lamb rib chops, about 2 inches thick (about 2 lbs. *total*)

Tapenade (recipe follows)

1 With a sharp knife, cut through fat on edges of chops at 1-inch intervals. Lay chops, fat sides up, on edge (they can lean against one another for support) in a shallow rimmed 10- by 15-inch baking pan. Broil 3 inches below heat until fat is lightly browned (8 to 10 minutes). Remove from oven.

2 Meanwhile, prepare Tapenade.

3 Drain and discard any fat from pan. Lay chops flat, well apart; firmly pat 1 tablespoon of the relish onto meaty part of each chop. Turn chops, over and coat with 1 more tablespoon of the relish. Bake in a 500° oven until rare in center when cut (about 10 minutes) or until done to your liking. Serve chops with remaining relish.

makes 2 or 4 servings

TAPENADE

Measure ½ cup oil-cured black ripe olives; cut meat from pits. (Or use ½ cup drained canned and pitted black ripe olives.) In a food processor or blender, combine olives, ¼ cup drained capers, 2 teaspoons Dijon mustard, 5 drained canned anchovy fillets, ¼ teaspoon each cracked bay leaves and dry thyme, and 1 large clove garlic, minced or pressed. Whirl until mixture is finely chopped but not puréed.

per serving: 251 calories, 25 g protein, 2 g carbohydrates, 16g total fat, 88 mg cholesterol, 951 mg sodium

quick meat sauce & green beans

preparation time: about 40 minutes

1 can (2 oz.) anchovy fillets

2 tablespoons olive oil or salad oil

1 medium-size onion, finely chopped

1 pound lean ground beef or lamb

1 can (14½ oz.) pear-shaped tomatoes

¼ pound cooked ham, finely chopped

1 tablespoon drained capers

¼ teaspoon crushed red pepper

1 to 1½ pounds green beans

⅓ cup grated Parmesan cheese

1 Drain anchovies and mince all but 3 of them; set aside.

2 Heat oil in a wide frying pan over medium-high heat; add onion and cook, stirring often, until soft (about 5 minutes). Crumble meat into pan; cook, stirring, until meat is well browned (10 to 12 minutes). Spoon off and discard excess fat. Add tomatoes (break up with a spoon) and their liquid, minced anchovies, ham, capers, and pepper. Boil gently, stirring often, until sauce is thickened (about 15 minutes). Meanwhile, cook beans, uncovered, in a large quantity of boiling salted water until tender-crisp (5 to 8 minutes); drain well.

3 Arrange beans on a platter. Top with sauce, sprinkle with cheese, and garnish with reserved whole anchovies.

makes 4 servings

per serving: 464 calories, 36 g protein, 17g carbohydrates, 29 g total fat, 98 mg cholesterol, 960 mg sodium

pork tenderloin with bulgur

preparation time: about 40 minutes

3 cups beef broth

1 cup bulgur (cracked wheat)

½ cup sliced green onions

1½ pounds pork tenderloin (about 2 tenderloins), trimmed of fat

2 teaspoons sugar

1 tablespoon vegetable oil

1 tablespoon mustard seeds

1 tablespoon balsamic vinegar

2 teaspoons minced fresh oregano or 1 teaspoon dried oregano

½ cup dry red wine

2 teaspoons cornstarch mixed with 2 teaspoons cold water

1 pound asparagus, tough ends broken off

Salt and pepper

1 In a 2- to 3-quart pan, bring 2 cups of the broth to a boil; stir in bulgur. Cover, remove from heat, and let stand until bulgur is tender to bite (about 30 minutes). Stir in onions.

2 While bulgur is standing, sprinkle pork with sugar. Heat oil in a wide frying pan over medium-high heat; add pork and cook, turning as needed, until browned on all sides (about 4 minutes). Add ⅔ cup of the broth, mustard seeds, vinegar, and oregano. Cover, reduce heat to medium-low, and simmer just until meat is no longer pink in center; cut to test (about 12 minutes).

3 Lift pork to a warm platter and keep warm. To pan, add wine and remaining ⅓ cup. Bring to a boil over high heat; then boil until reduced to ¾ cup (about 2 minutes). Stir in cornstarch mixture; return to a boil, stirring.

4 While sauce is boiling, bring ½ inch of water to a boil in anoth-er wide frying pan over high heat. Add asparagus and cook, uncovered, just until barely tender when pierced (about 4 minutes). Drain.

5 Slice pork; mound bulgur alongside, then top with asparagus. Spoon sauce over meat. Season to taste with salt and pepper.

makes 4 servings

per serving: 442 calories, 45 g protein, 36 g carbohydrates, 11 g total fat, 111 mg cholesterol, 1,327 mg sodium

spicy pork tenderloins

preparation time: about 30 minutes
marinating time: at least 4 hours

¼ cup *each* honey and prepared mustard

¼ teaspoon *each* salt and chili powder

2 pork tenderloins (about ¾ lb. *each*), fat and silvery membrane trimmed

1 In a large bowl, stir together honey, mustard, salt, and chili powder. Add pork, turning to coat. Cover and refrigerate for at least 4 hours or until next day, turning meat several times.

2 Lift out pork and drain, reserving marinade. Place pork on a lightly greased grill 4 to 6 inches above a solid bed of medium-hot coals. Cook, basting once with reserved marinade, until no longer pink in center (cut to test) or until a meat thermometer inserted in center registers 155° (about 20 minutes). Cover with foil and let stand for 10 minutes; cut across grain into thin, slanting slices.

makes 6 servings

per serving: 201 calories, 26 g protein, 12 g carbohydrates, 5g total fat, 84 mg cholesterol, 283 mg sodium

cuban style mini roast with black beans & rice

preparation time: about 1 1/4 hours
marinating time: at least 4 hours

1 1/2 to 1 3/4 pounds boneless fresh leg of pork, trimmed of fat

2 cloves garlic, minced or pressed

1/2 teaspoon dry oregano

1/4 teaspoon each cumin seeds (coarsely crushed) and crushed red pepper flakes

1/4 cup lime juice

Cuban Black Beans (recipe follows)

3 cups hot cooked long-grain white rice

1/4 cup thinly sliced green onions

Lime wedges

1 Roll pork compactly; then tie securely with cotton string at 1 1/2-inch intervals. Set a large heavy-duty plastic bag in a shallow pan. In bag, combine garlic, oregano, cumin seeds, red pepper flakes, and lime juice; add pork. Seal bag and turn to coat pork with marinade; then refrigerate for at least 4 hours or up to 1 day, turning occasionally.

2 Lift pork from bag and drain briefly; reserve marinade. Place pork on a rack in a roasting pan and roast in a 350° oven, drizzling once or twice with marinade, until a meat thermometer inserted in thickest part registers 155° (35 to 55 minutes). After 25 minutes, check temperature every 5 to 10 minutes. Meanwhile, prepare Cuban Black Beans.

3 When pork is done, let it stand for about 5 minutes. Then thinly slice pork across the grain and transfer to a platter. Spoon rice alongside pork. Garnish pork and rice with green onions and lime wedges; serve with Cuban Black Beans.

CUBAN BLACK BEANS

Heat 2 teaspoons olive oil in a wide nonstick frying pan over medium heat. Add 1 medium-size onion, thinly sliced, and 1/2 cup finely chopped green bell pepper; cook, stirring often, until onion is soft but not browned (about 5 minutes). Stir in 1 clove garlic, minced or pressed, 1/2 teaspoon ground cumin, and 1 can (about 15 oz.) black beans and their liquid. Cook, stirring, until heated through (about 3 minutes). Just before serving, stir in 2 teaspoons cider vinegar.

makes 6 servings

per serving: 435 calories, 34 g protein, 43 g carbohydrates, 12 g total fat, 87 mg cholesterol, 338 mg sodium

FAT LOWERING STRATEGIES FOR HIGHER-FAT MEAT: When you're confronted with a cut of meat other than low-fat cuts for which recipes are given, here are some ways you can prepare the meat in order to reduce unwanted fat.

- Trim surface fat scrupulously.
- Cook the meat in a way that renders the intramuscular fat. For example, you can pour off and discard the drippings that remain after browning meats for stew or pot roast or ground meat dishes.
- Skim and discard fat from the roasted meat drippings before adding liquid to roasting pan to make gravy or sauce.
- Make stews and soups ahead so that you can refrigerate them until thoroughly chilled. The fat that rises to the surface and hardens is then easier to lift off and discard, leaving a leaner dish to reheat.

gingered butterflied lamb with yams

preparation time: about 1½ hours
marinating time: at least 4 hours

⅓ cup chopped fresh ginger

8 cloves garlic, peeled

¼ teaspoon pepper

1½ tablespoons reduced-sodium soy sauce

¾ cup red wine vinegar

2 to 2½ pounds boneless butterflied leg of lamb, trimmed of fat

2 teaspoons sugar

¼ cup raisins

Vegetable oil cooking spray

8 to 10 small yams or sweet potatoes (3½ to 4 lbs., *total*), scrubbed

8 to 10 small onions (*each* about 2 inches in diameter), unpeeled, cut lengthwise into halves

1 cup beef broth

1 In a blender or food processor, combine ginger, garlic, pepper, soy sauce, and 2 tablespoons of the vinegar. Whirl until mixture forms a paste; set aside.

2 Lay lamb flat in 9- by 13-inch baking dish; spoon ginger mixture around lamb. Mix sugar, raisins, and remaining 10 tablespoons vinegar; pour over lamb. Cover and refrigerate for at least 4 hours or up to 1 day.

3 Coat a 12- by 17-inch or larger roasting pan with cooking spray. Cut unpeeled yams lengthwise into ¾-inch-thick wedges. Arrange yams and onion halves (cut side down) in pan. Coat all vegetables with cooking spray. Roast on lower rack of a 425° oven for 15 minutes. Meanwhile, lift lamb from marinade and drain briefly; reserve marinade. Place lamb, boned side down, on a rack in a shallow baking pan.

4 After vegetables have roasted for 15 minutes, place lamb in oven on middle rack. Continue to roast both lamb and vegetables, basting lamb occasionally with marinade, for 30 minutes. Lift raisins from marinade and sprinkle over lamb. Drizzle vegetables with all but 3 tablespoons of the remaining marinade. Continue to roast until vegetables are tender when pierced and a meat thermometer inserted in thickest part of lamb registers 140° to 145° for medium-rare (10 to 15 more minutes).

5 Transfer lamb, onions, and yams to a platter; keep warm. To lamb cooking pan, add broth and reserved 3 tablespoons marinade; cook over medium heat, stirring to scrape browned bits free, until sauce is reduced to about ¾ cup. Pour into a small bowl.

6 To serve, thinly slice lamb across the grain. Serve lamb with yams, onions, and sauce.

makes 8 to 10 servings

per serving: 328 calories, 27 g protein, 41 g carbohydrates, 6 g total fat, 73 mg cholesterol, 282 mg sodium

veal curry with fruit

preparation time: about 1 hour

1 pound boneless veal loin, fat trimmed

2 tablespoons margarine

1 medium-size onion, finely chopped

1 large carrot, finely chopped

3 tablespoons all-purpose flour

1 ½ teaspoons curry powder

½ teaspoon ground coriander

¼ teaspoon *each* cardamom and white pepper

1 cup low-sodium chicken broth

½ cup lowfat (2%) milk

6 tablespoons dry sherry

2 small bananas

2 teaspoons lemon juice

2 cups hot cooked brown or white rice

1 cup sliced peaches, papaya, or apricots

½ cup golden raisins

1 Slice veal across grain into ½-inch-thick strips about 3 inches long. In a wide frying pan, melt margarine over medium-high heat. Add veal and cook, stirring often, until lightly browned (about 7 minutes); lift out and set aside.

2 Add onion and carrot to pan and cook, stirring, until lightly browned (about 5 minutes). Stir in flour, curry powder, coriander, cardamom, and pepper; cook for 1 minute. Stir in chicken broth, milk, and 4 tablespoons of the sherry; bring to a boil. Return veal to pan; reduce heat, cover, and simmer until veal is tender (about 25 minutes). Stir in remaining sherry.

3 Slice bananas; coat with lemon juice. Spoon rice onto individual plates. Top with curry. Offer with bananas, peaches, and raisins.

makes 4 servings

per serving: 495 calories, 30 g protein, 70 g carbohydrates, 12 g total fat, 93 mg cholesterol, 217 mg sodium

TOOLS FOR LIGHT COOKING:

Vegetable oil cooking spray prevents lean meat from sticking to the cooking pan or rack, whether you're cooking it in a frying pan, in a Dutch oven, or on the grill. For added flavor, use olive oil spray. Some cooks also like to spray a cooking oil on well-trimmed roasts to promote browning while adding only a whisper of fat.

A roasting rack elevates the roasting meat above any fatty drippings so that the meat doesn't reabsorb them. If you can find a rack covered with nonstick coating, it will be easier to clean.

Nonstick pans are a ready answer to the problem of how to cook lean meat in a scant amount of fat. A heavy pan is a good investment for the kitchen because it's less likely to warp, enabling meat to brown evenly. Frying pans with nonstick coatings are plentiful. Nonstick-coated roasting pans also have many advantages.

marinated daube of beef

preparation time: about 3 1/2 hours
marinating time: at least 8 hours

2 pounds beef eye of round, trimmed of fat
  and cut into 1-inch cubes

1 cup dry red wine

2 teaspoons olive oil

1/4 cup chopped parsley

1 dry bay leaf

1/2 teaspoon dry thyme

1/4 teaspoon ground white pepper

2 strips orange peel (*each* about 1/2 by 3 inches)

2 medium-size onions, thinly sliced

1 1/2 cups water

1 clove garlic, minced or pressed

4 medium-size carrots, cut into 1/4-inch-thick
  slanting slices

3 medium-size tomatoes (1 to 1 1/4 lbs. *total*),
  peeled and cut into thin wedges

8 ounces mushrooms, cut into quarters

1/3 Niçoise or pitted ripe olives

1 tablespoon cornstarch blended
  with 2 tablespoons cold water

Salt

12 small thin-skinned potatoes (*each* 1 1/2 to
  2 inches in diameter), steamed or baked

1 In a 2- to 3-quart bowl, combine beef, wine, oil, parsley, bay leaf, thyme, white pepper, and orange peel. Cover and refrigerate for at least 8 hours, turning occasionally.

2 Lift beef from marinade and drain briefly; reserve marinade. Place beef in a heavy 3 1/2- to 4-quart pan and add onions, 1/2 cup of the water, and garlic. Cover and cook over low heat, stirring occasionally, for 30 minutes. Uncover, increase heat to medium, and continue to cook, stirring occasionally, until almost all liquid has evaporated and drippings are browned (about 25 minutes). Stir in reserved marinade and remaining 1 cup water. Bring to a boil; then reduce heat, cover, and simmer for 45 minutes.

3 Stir in carrots and tomatoes; cover and cook for 30 minutes. Add mushrooms and olives; cover and continue to cook until beef is very tender when pierced (30 to 45 minutes). Blend in cornstarch mixture; increase heat to medium-high and cook, stirring, until sauce is bubbly and thickened. Season to taste with salt. Serve stew with potatoes.

makes 8 servings

per serving: 294 calories, 28 g protein, 29 g carbohydrates, 7 g total fat, 61 mg cholesterol, 138 mg sodium

QUICK WAYS TO COOK MEAT: There's more than one way to cook steak and other meats when time is short. Stir-fried and sautéed meats, for example, both cook in minutes. Heat the pan first, with a little oil or other fat to protect the finish. And don't add too much meat at once. If you crowd the pan, it will cool off too quickly to sear the meat and seal in its juices; instead, juices will be released and meat will turn out tough and dry. Broiling is a reliably speedy method for cooking steaks and chops. Preheat the broiler, so that the meat can begin to cook the moment you close the oven door.

cranberry port pot roast

preparation time: about 4 to 4 1/4 hours

1 beef eye of round roast or rump roast
(3 1/2 to 4 lbs.), trimmed of fat

1 tablespoon salad oil

1 can (about 14 1/2 oz.) beef broth

1 3/4 cups port

1/3 cup firmly packed brown sugar

2 packages (about 10 oz. *each*) frozen tiny onions

2 cups fresh or frozen cranberries

6 cups hot cooked eggless noodles

2 tablespoons cornstarch blended
with 3 tablespoons cold water

Salt and pepper

1 Rub beef all over with oil, place in a 10- by 14-inch roasting pan, and bake in a 450° oven until well browned (about 45 minutes), turning often. Then reduce oven temperature to 400°. Add broth and port to pan, cover tightly, and bake for 1 1/2 hours.

2 Mix sugar and onions into pan juices; cover tightly and bake for 1 more hour. Stir in cranberries; cover tightly and bake until beef is tender when pierced (about 30 more minutes).

3 Transfer beef to a platter; spoon noodles alongside. With a slotted spoon, ladle onions and cranberries onto noodles; keep warm. Skim and discard fat from pan juices; then bring juices to a boil over high heat. Stir in cornstarch mixture; cook, stirring, until sauce is bubbly and thickened. Season to taste with salt and pepper, then pour into a small bowl.

4 To serve, thinly slice beef across the grain. Accompany beef and noodles with sauce.

makes 10 to 12 servings

per serving: 363 calories, 37 g protein, 34 g carbohydrates, 9 g total fat, 84 mg cholesterol, 234 mg sodium

lean sirloin stroganoff

preparation time: about 25 minutes

2 to 3 teaspoons salad oil

1 pound boneless top sirloin steak, trimmed of
fat and cut into 1/8-inch-thick, bite-size strips

1/3 cup thinly sliced shallots or sweet red onion

8 ounces mushrooms, thinly sliced

1 package (about 9 oz.) fresh fettuccine or
8 ounces dry fettuccine

2 teaspoons Worcestershire

1/4 teaspoon sweet Hungarian paprika

1/8 teaspoon ground white pepper

1/4 cup dry vermouth

3/4 cup plain low-fat yogurt blended
with 1 tablespoon cornstarch

1/4 teaspoon sugar

Salt

Chopped parsley

1 Heat 1 teaspoon of the oil in a wide nonstick frying pan over medium-high heat. Add half the beef. Cook, stirring, just until meat is browned on all sides; remove from pan. Repeat with 1 more teaspoon oil and remaining beef. Set all beef aside.

2 Add shallots and mushrooms to pan; add 1 more teaspoon oil, if necessary. Cook, stirring, until almost all liquid has evaporated and mushrooms are browned.

3 Meanwhile, cook fettuccine in a 5- to 6-quart pan in about 3 quarts boiling water until just tender to bite (3 to 4 minutes for fresh pasta, 8 to 10 minutes for dry); or cook according to package directions. Drain pasta, pour onto a deep platter, and keep warm.

4 To mushroom mixture, add Worcestershire, paprika, white pepper, and vermouth. Blend in yogurt mixture and sugar. Cook, stirring, until sauce is bubbly and thickened. Return beef to pan and stir to coat; then cook, stirring, just until heated through. Season to taste with salt. Spoon beef mixture over pasta and sprinkle with parsley.

makes 4 servings

per serving: 435 calories, 36 g protein, 46 g carbohydrates, 10 g total fat, 147 mg cholesterol, 145 mg sodium

lemon-broiled flank steak with onions

preparation time: about 1 1/2 hours
marinating time: at least 2 hours

1 to 1 1/4 pounds flank steak, trimmed of fat

1 large onion, thinly sliced

1/3 cup lemon juice

1 teaspoon Italian herb seasoning
 or 1/4 teaspoon *each* dry basil, oregano,
 thyme, and marjoram leaves

1 teaspoon grated lemon peel

1 large clove garlic, minced or pressed

1/4 teaspoon coarsely ground pepper

2 teaspoons sugar

2 tablespoons soy sauce

1 tablespoon olive oil

Lemon wedges (optional)

Chopped parsley (optional)

1 Score steak on both sides about 1/8 inch deep in a 1-inch diamond pattern. In a shallow baking dish, spread half the onion; top with steak and add remaining onion. In a small bowl, stir together lemon juice, herb seasoning, lemon peel, garlic, pepper, sugar, and soy sauce. Pour over steak and onion. Cover and refrigerate for at least 2 hours or up to 8 hours.

2 Lift steak from dish, reserving marinade and onion. Place steak on a lightly greased rack in a broiler pan. Broil 3 to 4 inches below heat, turning once until browned; cut to test (8 to 10 minutes total for rare to medium).

3 Meanwhile, heat oil in a medium-size frying pan over medium-high heat. Add marinade and onion and bring to a boil. Cook, stirring often, until onion is soft and lightly browned and most of the liquid has evaporated (6 to 8 minutes). Slice steak thinly across grain at a slant. Spoon onions over top. Garnish with lemon wedges and parsley, if desired.

makes about 4 servings

per serving: 211 calories, 22 g protein, 6 g carbohydrates, 11 g total fat, 52 mg cholesterol, 483 mg sodium

grilled orange-coriander steak

preparation time: about 20 minutes
marinating time: at least 4 hours

1 teaspoon grated orange peel

1/4 cup orange juice

1 medium-size onion, minced

3 cloves garlic, minced or pressed

1/4 cup white wine vinegar

1 1/2 tablespoons ground coriander

1 teaspoon each cracked pepper and dry basil

1 1/2 pounds boneless beef top round
 (cut about 1 inch thick), trimmed of fat

Finely shredded orange peel

1 In a bowl, stir together grated orange peel, orange juice, onion, garlic, vinegar, coriander, pepper, and basil. Measure out 1/2 cup of this marinade; cover and refrigerate until serving time.

2 Pour remaining marinade into a shallow bowl; add beef and turn to coat. Cover and refrigerate for at least 4 hours or up to 1 day, turning beef over occasionally.

3 Lift beef from marinade and drain briefly; reserve marinade. Place beef on a lightly oiled grill 4 to 6 inches above a solid bed of medium coals. Cook, turning once and basting often with marinade, until done to your liking; cut to test (about 8 minutes for rare). Meanwhile, pour reserved 1/2 cup marinade into a small pan. Place over low heat; heat until steaming.

4 To serve, thinly slice beef across the grain. Garnish with shredded orange peel; accompany with heated marinade.

makes 6 servings

per serving: 775 calories, 28 g protein, 5 g carbohydrates, 4 g total fat, 71 mg cholesterol, 54 mg sodium

spinach meat loaf

preparation time: about 2 hours

1 large egg white

¼ cup evaporated skim milk

1 can (about 8 oz.) tomato sauce

1 ½ cups soft French bread crumbs

1 small onion, finely chopped

1 large potato, scrubbed and grated

1 clove garlic, minced or pressed

2 teaspoons Dijon mustard

¾ teaspoon dry oregano

¼ teaspoon pepper

1 pound *each* extra-lean ground beef and ground
   skinless turkey breast

1 package (about 10 oz.) frozen chopped spinach,
   thawed and squeezed dry

¼ cup grated Romano or Parmesan cheese

1 tablespoon *each* firmly packed brown sugar
   and red wine vinegar

1 ¼ teaspoons Worcestershire

1 In a large bowl, combine egg white, milk, and ½ cup of the tomato sauce; beat until well combined. Stir in bread crumbs, onion, potato, garlic, mustard, oregano, and pepper. Add beef and turkey; mix lightly. On a large sheet of plastic wrap, pat meat mixture into a 12-inch square. Distribute spinach over meat to within ½ inch of edges; sprinkle evenly with cheese.

2 Using plastic wrap to lift meat, roll up meat jelly roll style. Pinch seam and ends closed to seal in filling. Carefully place meat loaf, seam side down, in a shallow baking pan.

3 Bake meat loaf in a 350° oven for 1¼ hours. Meanwhile, in a small bowl, stir together sugar, vinegar, Worcestershire, and remaining tomato sauce until well blended. Set aside.

4 Remove pan from oven; spoon out and discard any drippings. Spoon tomato sauce mixture over meat loaf. Return to oven and continue to bake until meat is well browned (15 to 20 more minutes). With wide spatulas, carefully transfer meat loaf to a platter. Let stand for about 5 minutes before slicing.

makes 8 servings

per serving: 259 calories, 30 g protein, 28 g carbohydrates, 7 g total fat, 73 mg cholesterol, 418 mg sodium

veal stew with caraway

preparation time: about 2 hours

1 to 1 ½ pounds boneless veal shoulder,
   trimmed of fat and cut into 1-inch cubes

1 tablespoon salad oil

¼ teaspoon salt

⅛ teaspoon ground white pepper

1 large onion, finely chopped

½ cup dry white wine

2 teaspoons caraway seeds

1 can (about 14 ½ oz.) low-sodium chicken broth

2 medium-size carrots, chopped

3 to 4 cups hot cooked eggless noodles

Chopped parsley

1 In a wide 3½- to 4-quart pan, combine veal, oil, salt, white pepper, onion, and wine. Cover and cook over medium-low heat for 30 minutes. Uncover pan and stir in caraway seeds. Increase heat to medium and continue to cook, stirring occasionally, until almost all liquid has evaporated and onion is browned (15 to 20 minutes). Add broth and carrots to pan, stirring to scrape browned bits free.

2 Reduce heat to low, cover, and simmer until veal is tender when pierced (35 to 45 minutes). Increase heat to medium and cook, uncovered, stirring often, until sauce is slightly thickened (12 to 15 minutes). To serve, spoon stew over noodles; sprinkle with parsley.

makes 4 to 6 servings

per serving: 288 calories, 28 g protein, 27 g carbohydrates, 8 g total fat, 98 mg cholesterol, 252 mg sodium

grilled beef pocket sandwiches

preparation time: about 30 minutes
marinating time: at least 30 minutes

1 1/2 pounds lean tender beef steak such as top sirloin (cut about 1 inch thick), trimmed of fat

1 large clove garlic, peeled

1/2 small onion, cut into chunks

2 tablespoons *each* sugar, water, salad oil, and lemon juice

1/3 cup reduced-sodium soy sauce

2 large red bell peppers, seeded and cut into 1 1/2-inch squares

6 pita breads (*each* about 6 inches in diameter), cut into halves

2 cups lightly packed cilantro sprigs, rinsed and crisped

1 Cut beef into long slices about 1/4 inch thick. In a blender or food processor, combine garlic, onion, sugar, water, oil, lemon juice, and soy sauce; whirl until puréed. Pour into a bowl. Add beef and bell peppers; stir to coat with marinade. Then cover and refrigerate for at least 30 minutes or up to 1 day, stirring occasionally.

2 Drain marinade from beef and peppers; reserve marinade. Thread beef strips alternately with peppers on thin metal skewers. (To thread each beef strip, pierce one end of strip with skewer; then fold strip back and forth several times, piercing each time. Threaded meat will have a "rippled" look.) Place skewers on a grill 4 to 6 inches above a solid bed of medium-hot coals. Cook, turning often and basting with marinade, until beef is done to your liking; cut to test (about 4 minutes for medium-rare).

3 To eat, fill pita bread halves with beef, bell peppers, and cilantro sprigs.

makes 6 servings

per serving: 420 calories, 33 g protein, 44 g carbohydrates, 72 g total fat, 76 mg cholesterol, 911 mg sodium

szechuan beef

preparation time: about 25 minutes, plus 30 minutes to soak mushrooms

Cooking Sauce (recipe follows)

8 medium-size dried shiitake mushrooms (each about 2 inches in diameter)

1 pound lean top round steak

1 tablespoon salad oil

16 small dried hot red chiles

1 pound carrots, cut into thin 3-inch strips

4 cups bite-size pieces cauliflower

2 cans (about 8 oz. *each*) sliced bamboo shoots

2 cans (about 8 oz. *each*) sliced water chestnuts

1 Prepare sauce; set aside. Soak mushrooms in warm water to cover for 30 minutes; drain. Cut off and discard stems; squeeze caps dry and thinly slice. Cut steak into strips.

2 Heat oil in a wok or 12- to 14-inch frying pan over medium-high heat. Add chiles and stir until chiles just begin to char. Remove chiles from pan.

3 Add meat to pan and stir-fry until browned (1 1/2 to 2 minutes); remove with a slotted spoon and set aside. Add carrots, cauliflower, and mushrooms; stir-fry for 1 minute, then cover and cook until carrots and cauliflower are tender-crisp to bite (about 3 minutes). Drain bamboo shoots and water chestnuts, add to pan, and stir-fry for 1 more minute.

4 Return meat and chiles to pan; stir Cooking Sauce and add. Stir until sauce boils and thickens.

COOKING SAUCE

Mix 3 tablespoons reduced-sodium soy sauce, 1 1/2 tablespoons dry sherry, 1 tablespoon sugar, and 3/4 teaspoon cornstarch.

makes 6 servings

per serving: 300 calories, 24 g protein, 38 g carbohydrates, 9 g total fat, 43 mg cholesterol, 392 mg sodium

italian pork stew with polenta

preparation time: about 2 1/4 hours

1 1/2 **pounds lean boneless pork (cut from leg or shoulder), fat trimmed, cut into 1** 1/2**-inch chunks**

3 1/2 **cups water**

3/4 **pound small mushrooms, halved**

1 **large onion, chopped**

2 **cloves garlic, minced or pressed**

1 **can (28 oz.) pear-shaped tomatoes**

1 **cup dry red wine**

1/2 **teaspoon** *each* **dry rosemary and dry marjoram, dry oregano, and dry thyme leaves**

4 **cups low-sodium chicken broth**

2 **cups polenta**

1/2 **cup chopped Italian parsley**

Rosemary sprigs (optional)

1 Place pork and 1/2 cup of the water in a 5- to 6-quart pan. Cover and cook over medium-high heat for 10 minutes. Uncover and continue cooking, stirring, until juices have evaporated and meat is browned (about 5 more minutes). Add mushrooms, onion, and garlic; reduce heat to medium and cook, stirring often, until onion is soft (about 5 minutes).

2 Add tomatoes (break up with a spoon) and their liquid, wine, dry rosemary, marjoram, oregano, and thyme, stirring to loosen browned bits. Bring to a boil; reduce heat and simmer, partially covered, until pork is tender (about 1 1/2 hours).

3 About 30 minutes before stew is done, bring chicken broth and remaining water to a boil in a heavy 3- to 4-quart pan over high heat. Stir in polenta in a thin stream. Cook, stirring, until polenta begins to thicken; reduce heat to low and continue cooking, stirring often, until no longer grainy (20 to 25 minutes).

4 Spoon onto a platter and top with stew; sprinkle with parsley. Garnish with rosemary sprigs, if desired.

makes 6 servings

per serving: 399 calories, 31 g protein, 49 g carbohydrates, 8 g total fat, 77 mg cholesterol, 321 mg sodium

pakistani beef kebabs

preparation time: about 25 minutes
marinating time: at least 8 hours

1 **cup plain low-fat yogurt**

1 **small onion, finely chopped**

1 **clove garlic, minced or pressed**

1 **teaspoon grated fresh ginger or** 1/4 **teaspoon ground ginger**

1 **small dried hot red chile, crushed**

1/2 **teaspoon cumin seeds, coarsely crushed**

1/4 **teaspoon** *each* **ground nutmeg, ground cardamom, and salt**

1/8 **teaspoon** *each* **ground cinnamon, ground cloves, and coarsely ground pepper**

1 1/2 **pounds boneless top sirloin steak, trimmed of fat**

1 In a 2-quart bowl, combine yogurt, onion, garlic, ginger, chile, cumin, nutmeg, cardamom, salt, cinnamon, cloves, and pepper. Cut steak into 1-inch cubes; stir into yogurt mixture. Cover and refrigerate, stirring once or twice, for at least 8 hours or until next day.

2 Lift meat from marinade and thread onto 6 skewers (*each* about 9 inches long). Place on a lightly greased grill 4 to 6 inches above a solid bed of medium-hot coals. Cook, turning skewers as needed, until meat is browned on all sides (8 to 10 minutes total for rare to medium-rare).

makes 6 servings

per serving: 182 calories, 27 g protein, 2 g carbohydrates, 6 g total fat, 77 mg cholesterol, 116 mg sodium

marsala beef & couscous

cooking time: about 20 minutes

1 pound lean boneless top sirloin steak (about 1 in. thick), trimmed of fat and cut across grain into 1/8-by 2-inch strips

1/4 cup marsala

3 green onions

2 1/2 cups canned beef broth

1/8 teaspoon saffron threads, or to taste

1 can (about 14 oz.) artichoke hearts in water, drained

1 cup pitted bite-size dried prunes

1 cup dried apricots

1 package (about 10 oz.) dried couscous

1 tablespoon olive oil

2 teaspoons cornstarch blended with 1 tablespoon cold water

Salt and pepper

1 In a large bowl, combine steak and marsala; set aside. Cut onions into 1-inch lengths and sliver lengthwise; set aside.

2 In a 4- to 5-quart pan, bring broth, saffron, artichokes, prunes, and apricots to a boil over high beat. Stir in couscous. Cover pan, remove from heat, and let stand until liquid has been absorbed (about 5 minutes).

3 While couscous stands, heat oil in a wide nonstick frying pan over medium-high heat. When oil is hot, lift meat from marinade and drain briefly (reserve marinade). Add meat to pan and cook, stirring, until done to your liking, cut to test (2 to 3 minutes for rare). With a slotted spoon, transfer near to a bowl; keep warm.

4 Stir cornstarch mixture well; pour into pan along with reserved marinade and any meat juices in bowl. Cook, stirring, until sauce boils and thickens slightly (about 1 minute). Remove pan from heat and stir in meat and onions. Transfer couscous to a platter, fluffing with a fork; top with meat mixture. Add salt and pepper to taste.

makes 6 servings

per serving: 456 calories, 25 g protein, 72 g carbohydrates, 6 g total fat, 46 mg cholesterol, 737 mg sodium

blackened steak with beans & greens

preparation time: about 25 minutes

3/4 pound top sirloin steak (about 1 in. thick), fat trimmed

1 tablespoon Cajun or blackening spice blend

1/2 cup salsa

1/2 cup nonfat sour cream

2 tablespoons lime juice

3/4 pound prewashed spinach leaves

1 can (about 15 oz.) black beans, rinsed and drained

1 jar (about 7.25 oz.) peeled roasted red peppers, drained and cut into thin strips

1 Pat steak with spice blend to coat both sides evenly. Heat a wide frying pan over medium-high heat. When pan is very hot, add steak. Cook, turning occasionally, until meat is well browned on the outside and done to your liking (cut to test; about 14 minutes for medium-rare.)

2 Meanwhile, in a blender or food processor, whirl salsa, sour cream, and lime juice until smooth. Arrange spinach, beans, and peppers decoratively on a large platter.

3 When meat is done, cut it into thin bite-size slices; add to platter. At the table, toss with salsa mixture. Add pepper to taste.

makes 4 servings

per serving: 247 calories, 27 g protein, 22 g carbohydrates, 5 g total fat, 52 mg cholesterol, 1,370 mg sodium

chile beef burritos

preparation time: about 30 minutes

1 fresh jalapeño or other small fresh hot chile, seeded and minced

2 cloves garlic, minced or pressed

$1/4$ to $1/2$ teaspoon ground red pepper (cayenne)

1 tablespoon reduced-sodium soy sauce

$1/2$ teaspoon sugar

1 pound lean boneless top sirloin steak (about 1 inch thick), trimmed of fat and cut across the grain into $1/8$- by 2-inch strips

4 to 8 low-fat flour tortillas (*each* 7 to 9 inches in diameter)

1 large onion, thinly sliced

1 teaspoon olive oil

1 In a large bowl, stir together chile, garlic, red pepper, soy sauce, and sugar. Add steak and stir to coat. Set aside.

2 Brush tortillas lightly with hot water; then stack, wrap in foil, and heat in a 350° oven until warm (10 to 12 minutes).

3 Meanwhile, in a wide nonstick frying pan or wok, combine onion and $1/4$ cup water. Stir-fry over medium-high heat until onion is soft and liquid has evaporated (4 to 5 minutes). Add oil; then stir in meat and its marinade. Stir-fry until meat is done to your liking; cut to test (2 to 3 minutes for rare).

4 To serve, spoon meat mixture into tortillas. Offer a choice of condiments to add to taste.

makes 4 servings

per serving: 293 calories, 28 g protein, 34 g carbohydrates, 7 g total fat, 69 mg cholesterol, 488 mg sodium

grilled top sirloin with wine-shallot sauce

preparation time: about 30 minutes

1 to $1 1/2$ pounds boneless top sirloin steak ($1 1/2$ to 2 inches thick), trimmed of fat

2 or 3 small red onions, unpeeled, cut in half lengthwise

1 tablespoon margarine

$1/2$ cup chopped shallots

$3/4$ cup dry red wine

1 tablespoon Dijon mustard

1 teaspoon Worcestershire

$1/2$ teaspoon *each* coarsely ground pepper and dry tarragon leaves

Salt

1 Place steak on a lightly greased grill 4 to 6 inches above a solid bed of medium coals. Place onions, cut sides down, on grill. Cook, turning both steak and onions after about 10 minutes, until a thermometer inserted in thickest part of steak registers 135° to 140° for rare and onions are soft when pressed (18 to 20 minutes total).

2 Meanwhile, melt margarine in a small, metal-handled frying pan on grill; add shallots and cook, stirring occasionally, until tinged with brown (6 to 8 minutes). Add wine, mustard, Worcestershire, pepper, and tarragon. Cook, stirring often, until sauce is reduced to about $1/2$ cup (about 10 minutes); then move to a cooler part of grill.

3 Transfer steak and onions to a platter. Slice steak thinly across grain at a slant. If desired, stir accumulated meat juices into sauce. Season sauce to taste with salt and spoon over steak and onions.

makes 4 to 6 servings

per serving: 231 calories, 27 g protein, 9 g carbohydrates, 9 g total fat, 76 mg cholesterol, 189 mg sodium

chayote with spiced lamb filling

preparation time: about 1 1/4 hours

3 chayotes (about 3/4 lb. *each*)

1 pound lean lamb sirloin, freshly ground

1 medium-size onion, minced

4 cloves garlic, minced or pressed

1/2 teaspoon *each* ground allspice and coarsely ground pepper

1/8 teaspoon ground cloves

1/3 cup raisins

1 can (6 oz.) tomato paste

2 tablespoons dry red wine

Similar in taste to zucchini, chayote is a tropical summer squash sometimes called mirliton. For an unusual entrée, serve it stuffed with a lightly spiced lamb filling.

1 In a 4- to 5-quart pan, bring 2 quarts water to a boil over high heat. Add chayotes; reduce heat, cover, and simmer until tender when pierced (about 40 minutes). Drain and let cool; halve lengthwise and discard pit. Scoop out and reserve pulp, leaving 1/2-inch-thick shells. Invert shells on paper towels to drain. Chop pulp.

2 Meanwhile, crumble lamb into a wide frying pan; add onion, garlic, allspice, pepper, and cloves. Cook over medium-high heat, stirring occasionally, until lamb is well browned (about 15 minutes). Stir in chayote pulp, raisins, tomato paste, and wine.

3 Spoon lamb mixture into shells. Place in a 9- by 13-inch baking pan. Cover and bake in a 350° oven for 20 minutes; uncover and continue baking until hot (about 5 more minutes).

makes 6 servings

per serving: 199 calories, 19 g protein, 23 g carbohydrates, 5 g total fat, 50 mg cholesterol, 281 mg sodium

grilled beef with soy seasoned sake

preparation time: about 40 minutes

1 1/2 pounds boneless beef top round (about 2 inches thick), trimmed of fat

1 tablespoon Asian sesame oil or salad oil

2 cloves garlic, minced or pressed

2 tablespoons grated fresh ginger

1/2 cup thinly sliced green onions (including tops)

2/3 cup sake or dry sherry

3 tablespoons soy sauce

12 green onions, ends trimmed

Salt and pepper

1 Place beef on a lightly greased grill 4 to 6 inches above a solid bed of medium hot coals. Cook, turning once, until beef is browned and a meat thermometer inserted in thickest part registers 135° to 140° for rare to medium-rare (20 to 25 minutes total).

2 Meanwhile, in a metal-handled 6- to 8-inch frying pan, combine oil, garlic, ginger, and sliced green onions; place on grill over coals. Cook, stirring often, until onions are limp (5 to 8 minutes). Add sake and soy sauce. Continue cooking, stirring once or twice, until mixture boils; then move to a cooler part of the grill.

3 When beef is almost done, lay whole green onions on grill and cook, turning once, until lightly browned (2 to 4 minutes total). Transfer beef and whole onions to a serving board; slice beef thinly across grain. Top with warm green onion sauce. Season to taste with salt and pepper.

makes 6 servings

per serving: 232 calories, 28 g protein, 7 g carbohydrates, 7 g total fat, 72 mg cholesterol, 571 mg sodium

spicy lamb skewers with baked lemon pilaf

preparation time: about 2 hours
marinating time: at least 3 hours

1 large onion, finely chopped

1 teaspoon salad oil

3 tablespoons cider vinegar

1 tablespoon curry powder

1 dry bay leaf

2 teaspoons chili powder

½ teaspoon salt

1 clove garlic, minced or pressed

¾ cup apricot nectar

2 pounds boneless lamb loin, trimmed of fat and cut into 1-inch cubes

Baked Lemon Pilaf (recipe follows)

1 In a medium-size pan, combine onion, oil, and vinegar. Cook over medium-low heat, stirring, until almost all liquid has evaporated and onion is soft (6 to 8 minutes). Stir in curry powder, bay leaf, chili powder, salt, garlic, and apricot nectar. Bring to a boil over high heat; then reduce heat to low and simmer for 5 minutes.

2 Place lamb in a bowl, pour in apricot marinade, and stir to combine. Cover and refrigerate for at least 3 hours or up to 8 hours, stirring occasionally. About 1 hour before cooking lamb, prepare Baked Lemon Pilaf.

3 Lift lamb from marinade and drain briefly; reserve marinade. Thread lamb on 8 metal skewers. Place skewers on an oiled grill 4 to 6 inches above a solid bed of hot coals. Cook, brushing with remaining marinade and turning as needed, until lamb is well browned on outside but still pink in center; cut to test (8 to 10 minutes). Serve with pilaf.

BAKED LEMON PILAF

Coat a deep 2-quart baking dish with vegetable oil cooking spray. Add 3 cups low-sodium chicken broth, 1½ cups long-grain white rice, 1 tablespoon grated lemon peel, 3 table-spoons lemon juice, ⅓ cup thinly sliced green onions, and 2 teaspoons butter or margarine. Stir to blend well. Cover baking dish tightly and bake in a 350° oven until rice is tender to bite (45 to 50 minutes). Fluff with a fork before serving.

makes 8 servings

per serving: 347 calories, 78 g protein, 34 g carbohydrates, 10 g total fat, 79 mg cholesterol, 194 mg sodium

BUY THE RIGHT AMOUNT: Though appetites vary, as a general rule you can allow ¼ to ⅓ pound per serving of lean, boneless meat with little or no fat, such as ground meat, flank steak, and fillets. For steaks and chips—meat with a medium amount of bone and some edge fat—allow about ½ pound per serving. For very bony cuts such as prime rib bones, allow a full pound per serving.

souvlaki in pitas

preparation time: about 25 minutes
marinating time: at least 30 minutes

1 pound lean top round steak
    (about 1 inch thick), fat trimmed

1/4 cup *each* lemon juice and dry white wine

2 cloves garlic, minced or pressed

1 teaspoon ground cumin

Souvlaki Sauce (recipe follows)

8 whole wheat pita breads (6-inch diameter)

Nonstick cooking spray or salad oil

2 large tomatoes (about 1 lb. *total*),
    cut into thin wedges

2 cups shredded romaine lettuce

1 small red onion (about 1/4 lb.),
    cut into thin rings

1 Slice steak across grain into long, 1/2-inch-thick strips. In a medium-size bowl, mix lemon juice, wine, garlic, and cumin. Add steak, turning to coat. Cover and refrigerate for at least 30 minutes or until next day: Meanwhile, prepare Souvlaki Sauce.

2 Wrap pita breads, 4 at a time, in foil; place in a 250° oven until warm (about 10 minutes).

3 Meanwhile, lightly coat a broiler pan rack with cooking spray. Drain steak and place on rack. Broil 3 to 4 inches below heat, turning once, until lightly browned but still juicy; cut to test (5 to 7 minutes total).

4 Place 2 or 3 pieces of meat in center of each pita bread. Top with sauce, tomatoes, lettuce, and onion and fold up.

SOUVLAKI SAUCE

Stir together 1 cup plain lowfat yogurt, 1 teaspoon dry oregano leaves, and 2 tablespoons water. Cover and refrigerate for at least 30 minutes or until next day.

makes 4 servings (2 Souvlaki each)

per serving: 560 calories, 42 g protein, 82 g carbohydrates, 8 g total fat, 70 mg cholesterol, 831 mg sodium

stir-fried beef & asparagus

preparation time: about 25 minutes

1/2 cup dry red wine

1/4 cup orange juice

2 tablespoons raspberry or red wine vinegar

1/4 cup finely chopped shallots

2 teaspoons chopped fresh tarragon or
    1/2 teaspoon dried tarragon

1 pound lean boneless top sirloin steak (about
    1 inch thick), trimmed of fat and cut across
    the grain into 1/8- by 2-inch strips

1 1/2 pounds asparagus

1 teaspoon olive oil

About 1/2 cup fresh raspberries

1 In a large bowl, stir together wine, orange juice, vinegar, shallots, and tarragon. Add steak and stir to coat. Set aside; stir occasionally.

2 Snap off and discard tough ends of asparagus; then cut spears into 3-inch lengths. Place asparagus and 1/2 cup water in a wide nonstick frying pan or wok. Cover; cook over medium-high heat, stirring occasionally, until asparagus is tender-crisp to bite (4 to 5 minutes). Drain asparagus, transfer to a platter, and keep warm. Wipe pan dry (be careful; pan is hot).

3 Heat oil in pan over medium-high heat. When oil is hot, lift meat from marinade and drain; reserve 1/4 cup of the marinade. Add meat to pan and stir-fry until done to your liking; cut to test (2 to 3 minutes for rare). Add the reserved 1/4 cup marinade and bring to a boil. Spoon meat mixture over asparagus; top with raspberries.

makes 4 servings

per serving: 213 calories, 27 g protein, 8 g carbohydrates, 6 g total fat, 69 mg cholesterol, 70 mg sodium

green chili with white beans

preparation time: about 2 1/2 hours

3 tablespoons salad oil

2 large green bell peppers, seeded and thinly sliced crosswise

2 cups sliced green onions (including tops)

8 cloves garlic, minced or pressed

4 teaspoons ground cumin

6 cans (13 oz. *each*) tomatillos

4 large cans (7 oz. *each*) diced green chiles

6 cans (15 oz. *each*) Italian white kidney beans (cannellini), drained; or 3 cups cooked small white beans, drained

3 pounds lean boneless pork shoulder or butt, trimmed of fat and cut into 1/2-inch cubes

4 teaspoons dry oregano leaves

1/2 teaspoon ground red pepper (cayenne)

1/2 cup lightly packed fresh cilantro leaves

1 Heat oil in a 10- to 12-quart pan over medium-high heat; add bell peppers, onions, garlic, and cumin. Cook, stirring, until onions are soft (about 5 minutes). Mix in tomatillos (break up with a spoon) and their liquid, chiles, beans, pork, oregano, and red pepper.

2 Bring to a boil; then reduce heat and simmer, stirring occasionally, until pork is tender when pierced (about 1 3/4 hours). For a thin chili, cook covered; for thicker chili, cook uncovered to desired consistency. Reserve a few cilantro leaves; chop remaining leaves. Stir chopped cilantro into chili; garnish with reserved leaves.

makes 12 servings

per serving: 441 calories, 36 g protein, 44 g carbohydrates, 14 g total fat, 76 mg cholesterol, 1231 mg sodium

marsala & mushroom steaks

preparation time: about 20 minutes

2 teaspoons margarine

1/2 pound mushrooms, sliced

vegetable oil cooking spray

2 beef tenderloin steaks (about 8 oz. *total*), trimmed of fat

Salt and pepper

3 tablespoons Marsala

Watercress sprigs, washed and crisped

1 In a wide nonstick frying pan, melt margarine over medium-high heat. Add mushrooms and cook, stirring often, until liquid has evaporated and mushrooms are browned (6 to 8 minutes). Lift mushrooms from pan and keep warm. Coat pan with cooking spray. Add steaks and cook, turning once, until well browned (4 to 6 minutes total for rare to medium rare). Place steaks on a warm platter and season to taste with salt and pepper; then top with mushrooms.

2 Add Marsala to drippings in pan and bring to a boil, stirring to loosen any browned bits. Spoon Marsala mixture over steaks and mushrooms. Garnish with watercress.

makes 2 servings

per serving: 282 calories, 26 g protein, 8 g carbohydrates, 24 g total fat, 70 mg cholesterol, 722 mg sodium

mediterranean veal ragout

preparation time: about 1 hour

1 pound lean boneless veal stew meat (cut from leg or shoulder), fat trimmed, cut into 1-inch chunks

2 medium-size onions, thinly sliced

$1/2$ cup water

1 teaspoon olive oil (preferably extra virgin)

1 cup low-sodium chicken broth

2 pound tomatoes, finely chopped

3 cloves garlic, minced or pressed

2 teaspoons dry thyme leaves

$1/2$ teaspoon dry rosemary

1 package (9 oz.) frozen artichoke hearts, thawed

2 tablespoons drained and rinsed capers

$1/2$ teaspoon anchovy paste or 1 teaspoon chopped canned anchovy fillets (optional)

1 tablespoon red wine vinegar

1 In a 5- to 6-quart pan, bring veal, onions, water, and oil to a boil over high heat; reduce heat, cover, and simmer, stirring occasionally, for 30 minutes.

2 Uncover, increase heat to medium-high, and cook, stirring often, until veal is lightly browned and onions begin to caramelize (about 5 minutes).

3 Add chicken broth, stirring to loosen browned bits. Reserve $1/4$ cup of the tomatoes; add remaining tomatoes, garlic, thyme, rosemary, artichokes, capers, and, if desired, anchovy paste. Reduce heat, cover, and simmer until veal is tender and artichokes are hot (about 15 minutes). Stir in vinegar and reserved tomatoes.

makes 4 servings

per serving: 203 calories, 28 g protein, 14 g carbohydrates, 4 g total fat, 89 mg cholesterol, 236 mg sodium

steak mexicana

preparation time: about 35 minutes

2 teaspoons salad oil

1 small onion, finely chopped

1 canned California green chile, seeded and chopped

$1/4$ teaspoon *each* salt and ground cumin

$1 1/2$ cups peeled chopped tomatoes

1 pound boneless top sirloin steak (about $3/4$ inch thick), trimmed of fat

$1/4$ cup shredded jack cheese

Lime wedges

Cilantro sprigs

1 Heat oil in a wide nonstick frying pan over medium heat. Add onion, chile, salt, and cumin. Cook, stirring often, until onion is soft and beginning to brown (3 to 5 minutes). Stir in tomato; increase heat to medium-high and cook, stirring often, until most of the liquid has evaporated (6 to 8 minutes). Keep sauce warm.

2 Cut steak into 4 portions. Place on a rack in a broiler pan. Broil about 4 inches below heat, turning once, until browned (4 to 6 minutes total). Spoon tomato sauce over steaks and top with cheese; broil until cheese is melted (1 to 2 minutes). Garnish with lime wedges and cilantro.

makes 4 servings

per serving: 234 calories, 28 g protein 5 g carbohydrates, 11 g total fat, 82 mg cholesterol, 346 mg sodium

baked polenta with veal sauce

preparation time: about 1 1/2 hours

Baked Polenta (recipe follows)

1 teaspoon olive oil

1 small onion, finely chopped

1 small carrot, shredded

4 ounces mushrooms, cut into quarters

1 clove garlic, minced or pressed

2 teaspoons Italian herb seasoning: or 1/2 teaspoon *each* dry basil, dry marjoram, dry oregano, and dry thyme

1 pound lean ground veal

1 large can (about 28 oz.) pear-shaped tomatoes

1/4 cup tomato paste

1/2 cup dry white wine

Salt and pepper

Grated Parmesan cheese (optional)

1 Prepare Baked Polenta. While polenta is baking, combine oil, onion, carrot, mushrooms, garlic, and herb seasoning in a wide nonstick frying pan. Cook over medium-high heat, stirring often, until onion is soft (about 5 minutes). Crumble veal into pan and cook, stirring often, until it begins to brown. Cut up tomatoes; then add tomatoes and their liquid, tomato paste, and wine to pan. Bring to a boil. Adjust heat so mixture boils gently; cook, uncovered, stirring occasionally, until thickened (about 20 minutes). Season to taste with salt and pepper.

2 Spoon Baked Polenta into wide, shallow bowls and top with veal sauce. Offer cheese to add to taste, if desired.

BAKED POLENTA

In an oiled shallow 2-quart baking dish, stir together 4 cups low-sodium chicken broth, 1 1/4 cups polenta, 1/4 cup finely chopped onion, and 1 tablespoon olive oil. Bake in a 350° oven until liquid has been absorbed (40 to 45 minutes).

makes 4 to 6 servings

per serving: 397 calories, 25 g protein, 43 g carbohydrates, 22 g total fat, 74 mg cholesterol, 494 mg sodium

lamb with fruited couscous

preparation time: about 2 1/4 hours

1 tablespoon olive oil

1 pound boned leg of lamb, cut into 1-inch cubes

1 large onion, chopped

1 1/2 teaspoons ground coriander

1 teaspoon ground ginger

1/2 teaspoon ground cumin

1/4 teaspoon ground allspice

1 cinnamon stick

2 cups low-sodium chicken broth

1/4 cup apricot or orange muscat dessert wine

1 cup dried apricots

10 ounces dried couscous

1 Heat oil in a 5- to 6-quart pan over medium-high heat. Add lamb and cook, turning often, until well browned (about 8 minutes). Lift out and set aside.

2 Add onion to pan and cook, stirring often, until soft (about 5 minutes). Add coriander, ginger, cumin, allspice, cinnamon stick, broth, and lamb. Bring to a boil; reduce heat, cover, and simmer until lamb is tender when pierced (about 1 1/2 hours). Discard cinnamon stick. (At this point, you may cool, cover, and refrigerate for up to a day; discard fat and reheat to continue.)

3 Lift out lamb and place on a platter; keep warm. Skim off and discard fat from pan drippings (if not already done). Measure drippings. If less than 2 1/3 cups, add water, and return to pan; if more, boil over high heat until reduced to 2 1/3 cups. Add wine and apricots; bring to a boil. Stir in couscous; cover, remove from heat, and let stand until liquid is absorbed (about 5 minutes).

4 Mound couscous beside lamb.

makes 4 servings

per serving: 606 calories, 36 g protein, 89 g carbohydrates, 10 g total fat, 73 mg cholesterol, 112 mg sodium

barbequed sirloin with scorched corn & chile salsa

preparation time: about 35 minutes
marinating time: at least 2 hours

Cumin-Cinnamon Marinade (recipe follows)

1 pound boneless sirloin steak
   (about ³/₄ inch thick), trimmed of fat

1 small tomato, seeded and finely chopped

1 medium-size fresh Anaheim (California)
   green chile, seeded and finely chopped

2 cloves garlic, minced or pressed

2 tablespoons lime juice

1 tablespoon ground New Mexico
   or California chiles

2 medium-size ears corn

Salt

Lime slices

1 Prepare Cumin-Cinnamon Marinade; add steak. Cover and refrigerate for at least 2 hours or until next day. Shortly before cooking steak, combine tomato, chopped chile, garlic, lime juice, and ground chiles; set aside.

2 Remove and discard husks and silk from corn. Lift steak from bowl, reserving marinade. Place steak and corn on a lightly greased grill 4 to 6 inches above a solid bed of medium-hot coals. Cook, drizzling steak several times with marinade and turning once, and turning corn as needed, until both are browned (8 to 10 minutes total for rare to medium-rare steak, about 8 minutes total for corn).

3 Place steak on a carving board and keep warm. Cut corn from cobs and stir into tomato mixture; season to taste with salt. Slice or quarter steak and garnish with lime slices; serve with salsa.

CUMIN-CINNAMON MARINADE

In a shallow glass bowl, combine ¹/₂ cup dry red wine; 1 tablespoon olive oil; 2 tablespoons finely chopped onion; 2 cloves garlic, minced or pressed; ¹/₄ teaspoon salt; ¹/₂ teaspoon *each* ground cumin and ground cinnamon; and 1 ¹/₂ teaspoons cumin seeds.

makes 4 servings

per serving: 222 calories, 26 g protein, 13 g carbohydrates, 8 g total fat, 69 mg cholesterol, 148 mg sodium

sweet & sour flank steak

preparation time: about 25 minutes
marinating time: at least 4 hours

¹/₃ cup cider vinegar

¹/₄ cup *each* honey and reduced-sodium soy sauce

1 clove garlic, minced or pressed

¹/₈ teaspoon liquid hot pepper seasoning

1 ¹/₂ pounds flank steak, fat trimmed

Parsley sprigs (optional)

1 In a small pan, cook vinegar, honey, soy sauce, garlic, and hot pepper seasoning over medium heat, stirring often, until honey is dissolved and mixture is well blended (about 5 minutes). Let cool briefly.

2 Place steak in a shallow nonmetal bowl just large enough to hold it; pour in marinade. Cover and refrigerate for at least 4 hours or until next day, turning once or twice.

3 Lift out steak and drain, reserving marinade. Place on a lightly greased grill 4 to 6 inches above a solid bed of medium-hot coals. Cook, turning once and basting often with marinade, until done to your liking; cut to test (8 to 10 minutes total for rare).

4 Meanwhile, bring any remaining marinade to a boil in a small pan over high heat. Slice steak thinly across grain. Garnish with parsley, if desired, and offer with marinade.

makes 6 servings

per serving: 254 calories, 22 g protein, 14 g carbohydrates, 12 g total fat, 58 mg cholesterol, 473 mg sodium

hungarian beef stew

preparation time: about 2 1/2 hours

1 1/2 pounds boneless beef top round, trimmed of fat and cut into 1-inch cubes

1 can (about 14 1/2 oz.) beef broth

1 clove garlic, minced or pressed

1 tablespoon sweet Hungarian paprika

3 medium-size leeks (1 to 1 1/2 lbs. *total*)

1 large red bell pepper, seeded and cut into 1-inch squares

8 ounces small mushrooms

1/2 teaspoon salt

1/4 teaspoon pepper

2 tablespoons port or Madeira

1/2 cup plain low-fat yogurt blended with 1 tablespoon cornstarch

1 In a wide 3½- to 4-quart pan, combine beef and ½ cup of the broth. Cover and cook over medium heat for 30 minutes. Uncover, add garlic and paprika, and continue to cook, stirring occasionally, until almost all liquid has evaporated and drippings are browned (about 30 minutes).

2 Meanwhile, trim and discard ends and all but 1½ inches of green tops from leeks; remove tough outer leaves. Split leeks lengthwise; rinse well, then cut crosswise into 1-inch lengths. Set aside.

3 Blend remaining 1 ¼ cups broth into stew, stirring to scrape browned bits free. Mix in leeks, bell pepper, mushrooms, salt, and pepper. Bring to a boil; reduce heat, cover, and simmer until beef is very tender when pierced (about 1 hour).

4 When beef is done, stir port and yogurt mixture into stew. Increase heat to medium-high and bring to a boil; then boil, stirring, until sauce is bubbly and thickened.

makes 6 servings

per serving: 223 calories, 30 g protein, 14 g carbohydrates, 5 g total fat, 66 mg cholesterol, 507 mg sodium

rich brown braised beef

preparation time: 1 3/4 to 2 hours

2 pounds boneless beef round tip, trimmed of fat and cut into 1-inch cubes

2 cloves garlic, minced or pressed

1 tablespoon salad oil

2 cups water

2 tablespoons *each* low-sodium soy sauce, red wine vinegar, and grape jelly

1/4 teaspoon *each* pepper, paprika, and dry oregano

4 drops liquid hot pepper seasoning

1 pound dry medium-wide eggless noodles

1 1/2 teaspoons cornstarch blended with 1 tablespoon cold water

Salt

Chopped parsley

1 In a 3- to 3½ -quart pan, combine beef, garlic, oil, and ½ cup of the water. Cover and cook over medium heat for 30 minutes. Uncover and continue to cook, stirring occasionally, until almost all liquid has evaporated and drippings are browned (15 to 20 minutes). Stir in soy sauce, vinegar, jelly, pepper, paprika, oregano, hot pepper seasoning, and remaining 1 ½ cups water. Bring to a boil; then reduce heat, cover, and simmer until beef is very tender when pierced (about 45 minutes).

2 When beef is almost done, cook noodles in a 6- to 8-quart pan in about 4 quarts boiling water until just tender to bite (7 to 9 minutes); or cook according to package directions. Drain well, pour onto a deep platter, and keep warm.

3 Gradually stir cornstarch mixture unto stew. Increase heat to medium and cook, stirring occasionally, just until sauce is bubbly and thickened. Season to taste with salt. Spoon stew over noodles; sprinkle with parsley.

makes 8 servings

per serving: 373 calories, 32 g protein, 44 g carbohydrates, 7 g total fat, 68 mg cholesterol, 236 mg sodium

citrus-seasoned steak & brown rice

preparation time: about 1 1/2 hours
marinating time: at least 3 hours

1 teaspoon grated orange peel

1/2 teaspoon dry thyme

1/4 cup white wine vinegar

1 tablespoon salad oil

1/3 cup orange juice

2 1/2 pounds boneless beef top round (cut 1 1/2 to 2 inches thick), trimmed of fat

Brown Rice a l'Orange (recipe follows)

Salt

Orange slices

Sage sprigs

1 In a wide, shallow bowl, stir together orange peel, thyme, vinegar, oil, and 3 tablespoons of the orange juice. Add beef and turn to coat. Cover and refrigerate for at least 3 hours or up to 1 day, turning occasionally.

2 About 30 minutes before broiling beef, prepare Brown Rice a l'Orange. Lift beef from marinade and drain briefly; reserve marinade. Place beef on a rack in a broiler pan. Broil about 6 inches below heat, turning once and basting occasionally with marinade, until beef is well browned and a meat thermometer inserted in thickest part registers 120 to 125° for rare (20 to 25 minutes).

3 Transfer beef to a carving board and keep warm. Skim and discard fat from pan drippings, if necessary. Pour remaining orange juice into broiler pan and stir over medium heat until blended. Season pan juices to taste with salt.

4 To serve, cut beef across the grain into thin slanting slices. Garnish with orange slices and sage sprigs. Serve with Brown Rice a l'Orange; offer pan juices to spoon over beef and rice.

BROWN RICE A L'ORANGE

1 In a 3- to 3 1/2-quart pan, combine 2 cups orange juice, 1 cup *each* water and dry white wine, 5 sage sprigs (or 1/2 teaspoon dry sage), and 3 thin strips orange peel (*each* about 2 inches long).

2 Bring juice mixture to a boil over high heat; stir in 2 cups long-grain brown rice. Reduce heat, cover, and simmer until rice is tender to bite (45 to 50 minutes). Remove from heat; let stand, uncovered, for 5 minutes. Discard orange peel and sage sprigs; fluff rice with a fork.

makes 8 to 10 servings

per serving: 348 calories, 32 g protein, 39 g carbohydrates, 6 g total fat, 72 mg cholesterol, 30 mg sodium

crusted lamb & potatoes

preparation time: about 1 ³/₄ hours

3 pounds russet potatoes, peeled and cut into
  ³/₄-inch-thick slices

1 ¹/₂ cups low-sodium chicken broth

Upper thigh half (3 to 3 ¹/₂ lbs.) of 1 leg of lamb,
  trimmed of fat

Seasoning Paste (recipe follows)

Salt and pepper

1 Arrange potatoes over bottom of a 12- by 15-inch roasting pan; pour broth into pan, then set lamb on potatoes. Roast in a 400° oven for 45 minutes. Meanwhile, prepare Seasoning Paste.

2 Spread paste evenly over lamb and potatoes. Continue to roast until crust on meat is well browned and a meat thermometer inserted in thickest part of lamb at bone registers 140° to 145° for medium-rare (about 25 more minutes). Transfer lamb and potatoes to a platter; pour any pan juices over all.

3 To serve, slice lamb across the grain; season lamb and potatoes to taste with salt and pepper.

SEASONING PASTE

In a small bowl, mash together 3 cloves garlic, minced or pressed; 1 small onion, minced; 3 tablespoons minced parsley; 1 cup seasoned stuffing mix; 3 tablespoons butter or margarine, at room temperature; 1 tablespoon grated lemon peel; and 2 tablespoons lemon juice.

makes 6 servings

per serving: 482 calories, 39 g protein, 49 g carbohydrates, 74 g total fat, 16 mg cholesterol, 357 mg sodium

eye of round in caper sauce

preparation time: about 15 minutes

4 beef eye of round steaks, *each* about
  ¹/₂ inch thick (1 lb. *total*), trimmed of fat

About 1 tablespoon all-purpose flour

Olive oil cooking spray

1 teaspoon margarine

1 teaspoon *each* Dijon mustard and drained capers

1 tablespoon *each* lemon juice and chopped chives

1 Place steaks between sheets of plastic wrap and pound with flat side of a meat mallet until about ¹/₄ inch thick. Dust with flour, shaking off excess.

2 Spray a wide nonstick frying pan with cooking spray and place over medium-high heat. Cook steaks, turning once, until browned on both sides (2 to 3 minutes total). Transfer steaks to plates and keep warm.

3 Remove pan from heat and add margarine; stir in mustard, capers, and lemon juice. Drizzle caper sauce over steaks; garnish with chives.

makes 4 servings

per serving: 170 calories, 25 g protein, 2 g carbohydrates, 6 g total fat, 61 mg cholesterol, 128 mg sodium

side dishes

almond pilaf with sherry

preparation time: about 35 minutes

½ cup slivered blanched almonds

½ cup 1-inch lengths of dry vermicelli

¼ cup butter or margarine

1 cup long-grain white rice

1¼ cups regular-strength chicken broth

¾ cup cream sherry

1½ teaspoons dry tarragon or 1 tablespoon chopped fresh tarragon

Tarragon sprigs (optional)

FREEZING & REHEATING BREAD To freeze freshly baked bread or rolls, let cool completely; then wrap airtight in foil, package in a plastic bag, label, and place in the freezer for up to 3 months. To serve, unwrap but leave partially covered; let thaw completely at room temperature before serving or reheating. To reheat, place thawed bread on a baking sheet in a 350° oven. Heat rolls and small loaves of bread for about 10 minutes, large loaves for 15 minutes. If bread has a soft crust, protect it during reheating with a loose wrapping of foil; if bread is crusty, heat it uncovered.

1 Toast almonds in a wide frying pan over medium heat until golden brown (about 4 minutes), stirring. Remove from pan and set aside.

2 Add vermicelli to pan and stir until golden brown (about 2 minutes); remove from pan and set aside. Add butter and rice to pan; cook, stirring, until rice is lightly toasted (about 3 minutes). Add broth, sherry, dry tarragon, and vermicelli. Bring mixture to a boil; reduce heat, cover, and simmer until rice is tender to bite (about 20 minutes). Sprinkle with almonds and garnish with tarragon sprigs, if desired.

makes 6 servings

per serving: 303 calories, 7 g protein, 38 g carbohydrates, 14 g total fat, 21 mg cholesterol, 290 mg sodium

baked potato sticks

preparation time: about 35 minutes

2 large russet potatoes

2 to 3 tablespoons butter or margarine, melted

Garlic salt

Dry oregano

1 Scrub potatoes and cut each one lengthwise into eighths. Brush with butter; sprinkle with garlic salt and oregano. Arrange potato wedges, skin sides down, about 1 inch apart on a large baking sheet.

2 Bake in a 425° oven until tender when pierced (about 30 minutes).

makes 4 servings

per serving: 144 calories, 2 g protein, 18 g carbohydrates, 7 g total fat, 19 mg cholesterol, 81 mg sodium

BAKED SWEET POTATO STICKS

Follow directions for Baked Potato Sticks, but substitute 2 large sweet potatoes or yams for russet potatoes. Omit garlic salt and oregano; instead, sprinkle potatoes with ground nutmeg. Decrease baking time to 25 minutes.

makes 4 servings

per serving: 272 calories, 3 g protein, 48 g carbohydrates, 8 g total fat, 19 mg cholesterol, 99 mg sodium

shredded rutabagas

preparation time: 10 to 15 minutes

3 tablespoons butter or margarine

2 cups coarsely shredded, firmly packed rutabagas

2 tablespoons water

1 to 1½ tablespoons firmly packed brown sugar

1 teaspoon soy sauce

1 Melt butter in a wide frying pan over medium-high heat.

2 Add rutabagas, water, sugar, and soy sauce. Cover and cook, stirring often, until rutabagas are tender-crisp to bite (about 5 minutes).

makes 4 servings

per serving: 125 calories, 1 g protein, 11 g carbohydrates, 9 g total fat, 23 mg cholesterol, 192 mg sodium

wilted spinach with parmesan & pepper

preparation time: about 20 minutes

8 cups firmly packed stemmed, rinsed, and drained spinach leaves

1 tablespoon butter or margarine

¼ cup grated or shredded Parmesan cheese

Coarsely ground pepper

1 Place spinach (with water that clings to leaves) in a shallow 3-quart casserole; dot with butter. Cover and bake in a 450° oven until leaves are wilted (10 to 12 minutes).

2 Lightly mix spinach with 2 forks to coat with butter. At the table, offer cheese and pepper to season spinach to taste.

makes 4 servings

per serving: 81 calories, 6 g protein, 5 g carbohydrates, 5 g total fat, 13 mg cholesterol, 242 mg sodium

broiled tomatoes parmesan

preparation time: about 10 minutes

6 medium-size tomatoes

Pepper

Dry basil

2 tablespoons grated Parmesan cheese

2 tablespoons butter or margarine

1 Cut tomatoes in half crosswise. Sprinkle cut surfaces with pepper and basil; then sprinkle evenly with cheese and dot evenly with butter.

2 Place tomatoes, cut sides up, on rack of a broiler pan; broil about 6 inches below heat until lightly browned (3 to 4 minutes).

makes 6 servings

per serving: 65 calories, 2 g protein, 5 g carbohydrates, 5 g total fat, 12 mg cholesterol, 80 mg sodium

skillet squash

preparation time: about 20 minutes

3 tablespoons olive oil, butter, or margarine

1 clove garlic, minced or pressed

6 medium-size zucchini, cut crosswise into
¼-inch-thick slices

1 tablespoon *each* minced parsley and thinly
sliced green onion (including top)

1 teaspoon dry oregano

¼ teaspoon sugar

Salt and pepper

SHOP WISELY Cooks who enjoy food seasoned and cooked to their
own tastes aren't likely to accept completely prepared foods.
Rather than searching for a frozen entrée that measures up to
memories of traditional cooking, learn to identify the cuts of meat
and poultry that can be cooked to your taste in a short time.

1 Heat oil in a wide frying pan over medium-high heat. Add garlic;
cook, stirring, for 2 to 3 minutes.

2 Add zucchini and cook, stirring often, just until tender-crisp to bite (3
to 5 minutes).

3 Stir in parsley, onion, oregano, and sugar. Season to taste with salt and
pepper. Continue to cook, stirring, until zucchini and seasonings are
well blended (1 to 2 more minutes).

makes 4 to 6 servings

per serving: 102 calories, 2 g protein, 6 g carbohydrates, 8 g total fat, 0 mg cholesterol,
6 mg sodium

hashed-brown zucchini

preparation time: about 35 minutes

1½ pounds zucchini

½ teaspoon salt

2 eggs

6 tablespoons grated Parmesan cheese

1 clove garlic, minced or pressed

About ¼ cup butter or margarine

Tomato wedges (optional)

1 Coarsely shred zucchini (you should have about 4 cups) and combine
with salt in a medium-size bowl. Let stand for about 15 minutes.
Squeeze with your hands to press out moisture. Stir in eggs, cheese,
and garlic.

2 Melt 2 tablespoons of the butter in a wide frying pan over medium-
high heat. Mound about 2 tablespoons of the zucchini mixture in pan;
flatten slightly to make a patty. Repeat until pan is filled, but don't
crowd patties in pan. Cook patties, turning once, until golden on both
sides (about 6 minutes). Lift out and arrange on a warm platter; keep
warm. Repeat to cook remaining zucchini mixture, adding more butter
as needed. Garnish with tomatoes, if desired.

makes 4 servings

per serving: 197 calories, 8 g protein, 6 g carbohydrates, 16 g total fat, 143 mg cholesterol,
428 mg sodium

asparagus with orange-butter sauce

preparation time: about 35 minutes

2 pounds asparagus, tough ends removed

½ cup butter or margarine

⅓ cup minced shallots

1¼ teaspoons Dijon mustard

1⅓ cups fresh orange juice

Salt and pepper

Orange slices; or strips of orange peel
tied in knots (optional)

1 In a wide frying pan, bring 1½ inches water to a boil over high heat. Add asparagus; reduce heat, cover, and boil gently just until tender when pierced (5 to 7 minutes). Drain, place on a warm platter, and keep warm.

2 Melt 1 tablespoon of the butter in a 1- to 2-quart pan over medium heat. Add shallots and cook, stirring, for 1 minute. Add mustard and orange juice, increase heat to high, and bring to a boil; boil until reduced to ⅔ cup (about 5 minutes). Reduce heat to low, add remaining 7 tablespoons butter all at once, and cook, stirring constantly, until butter is smoothly blended into sauce. Season to taste with salt and pepper. Spoon sauce over asparagus; garnish with orange slices or orange peel, if desired.

makes 4 to 6 servings

per serving: 223 calories, 4 g protein, 12 g carbohydrates, 19 g total fat, 50 mg cholesterol, 229 mg sodium

broccoli polonaise

preparation time: about 20 minutes

1 to 1½ pounds broccoli

5 tablespoons butter or margarine

½ cup fine dry bread crumbs

1 hard-cooked egg, chopped

1 tablespoon *each* thinly sliced green onion
(including top) and minced parsley

1 Trim and discard tough stalk bases from broccoli; peel stalks, then cut broccoli lengthwise into uniform spears.

2 In a wide frying pan, bring 1 inch water to a boil over high heat. Add broccoli; then reduce heat, cover, and boil gently just until stalks are tender when pierced (7 to 12 minutes). Drain. While broccoli is cooking, melt butter in a small pan over medium heat. Add bread crumbs and stir until browned. Remove from heat; stir in egg, onion, and parsley. Sprinkle crumb mixture over hot broccoli.

makes 4 to 6 servings

per serving: 176 calories, 5 g protein, 11 g carbohydrates, 13 g total fat, 74 mg cholesterol, 222 mg sodium

roasted onion halves

preparation time: 35 to 50 minutes

3 large onions (each 3 to 3½ inches in diameter)

¼ cup balsamic or red wine vinegar

Butter or margarine

Salt and pepper

1 Cut unpeeled onions in half lengthwise. Pour vinegar into a 9- by 13-inch baking pan; place onions, cut sides down, in pan.

2 Roast in a 350° oven until onions are soft when pressed (30 to 45 minutes). To eat, scoop onions from skins; add butter, salt, and pepper to taste.

makes 6 servings

per serving: 62 calories, 1 g protein, 6 g carbohydrates, 4 g total fat, 10 mg cholesterol, 41 mg sodium

cheese & chile rice

preparation time: about 40 minutes

3 cups cooked long-grain white rice

1 can (4 oz.) diced green chiles

1 jar (2 oz.) diced pimientos, drained

1 cup sour cream

1 cup shredded jack cheese

1 cup shredded Cheddar cheese

1 In a large bowl, stir together rice, chiles, pimientos, sour cream, jack cheese, and ½ cup of the Cheddar cheese.

2 Pour mixture into a greased shallow 1½-quart casserole; sprinkle with remaining ½ cup Cheddar cheese.

3 Bake in a 350° oven until mixture is hot throughout and cheese is melted (about 30 minutes).

makes 6 servings

per serving: 390 calories, 14 g protein, 37 g carbohydrates, 20 g total fat, 53 mg cholesterol, 359 mg sodium

curried garbanzos

preparation time: about 40 minutes

3 tablespoons salad oil

1 large onion, finely chopped

3 cloves garlic, minced or pressed

1 tablespoon minced fresh ginger

1 large tomato, chopped

1½ teaspoons ground cumin

1 teaspoon ground coriander

½ teaspoon *each* ground red pepper (cayenne) and ground turmeric

2 cans (about 1 lb. *each*) garbanzos, drained

¾ cup water

2 large limes

¼ cup chopped fresh cilantro leaves (optional)

1 Combine oil, onion, garlic, and ginger in a wide frying pan. Cook over medium heat, stirring often, until onion is lightly browned. Add tomato and cook, stirring, until most of the liquid has evaporated. Add cumin, ground coriander, red pepper, and turmeric. Reduce heat to low and stir until spices become aromatic (3 to 5 minutes).

2 Add garbanzos and water. Cover and simmer, stirring occasionally, until sauce is thickened (about 20 minutes). Stir in juice from half a lime. Pour mixture into a bowl and sprinkle with chopped cilantro, if desired. Cut remaining lime, and offer wedges alongside.

makes 4 to 6 servings

per serving: 197 calories, 7 g protein, 23 g carbohydrates, 9 g total fat, 0 mg cholesterol, 407 mg sodium

oven-browned eggplant with herbs

preparation time: 30 to 50 minutes

1 large eggplant, unpeeled

3 tablespoons olive oil or salad oil

2 teaspoons dry basil, oregano, rosemary, or thyme

1 clove garlic, minced or pressed

Salt and pepper

1 Slice eggplant crosswise about ½ inch thick. Mix oil, basil, and garlic and lightly brush over cut surfaces of eggplant.

2 Place eggplant in a single layer in a shallow baking pan. Bake, uncovered, in a 425° oven until eggplant is browned and very soft when pressed (25 to 40 minutes); turn, if necessary, to brown evenly. Season with salt and pepper to taste.

makes 4 servings

per serving: 137 calories, 2 g protein, 11 g carbohydrates, 10 g total fat, 0 mg cholesterol, 7 mg sodium

tandoori roasted vegetables

preparation time: about 50 minutes

12 cups bite-size vegetables (see notes)

3 tablespoons olive oil

1½ tablespoons tandoori masala

Salt and pepper

notes: *Use a mixture of these vegetables in proportions desired, changing for variety each time you prepare dish: 1-inch bell pepper squares, ¼-inch-thick diagonal carrot and asparagus slices, whole cherry tomatoes, and ½-inch turnip or zucchini chunks. Serve as a first course or with roasted meats.*

1 In an 11- by 17-inch roasting pan, mix vegetables, oil, and tandoori masala.

2 Bake in a 400° oven, stirring occasionally, until vegetables are browned and tender when pierced, 40 to 45 minutes (30 to 35 minutes in a convection oven).

3 Transfer to serving dish. Serve hot or cool. Cover and chill up to 1 day. Add salt and pepper to taste.

makes 6 to 8 servings

per serving: 101 cal., 50% (50 cal.) from fat; 3.1 g protein; 5.6 g fat (0.7 g sat.); 12 g carbohydrates (3.4 g fiber); 45 mg sodium; 0 mg cholesterol

bacon polenta

preparation time: about 25 minutes

5 slices bacon, chopped

⅓ cup finely chopped onion

2 large cloves garlic, minced or pressed

2¼ cups regular-strength chicken broth

¾ cup polenta or yellow cornmeal

Salt

1 In a 3-quart pan, cook bacon over medium heat until lightly browned (about 5 minutes), stirring. Add onion and garlic and cook, stirring, until onion is soft and bacon is well browned (about 5 more minutes). Discard all but 1 tablespoon of the drippings.

2 Add 1½ cups of the broth to pan and bring to a boil over high heat. Meanwhile, in a small bowl, mix polenta with remaining ¾ cup broth. Using a long-handled spoon, stir polenta mixture into boiling broth (mixture will thicken and spatter). Reduce heat to low and cook, stirring constantly, for 5 minutes. Season to taste with salt.

makes 4 servings

per serving: 186 calories, 7 g protein, 22 g carbohydrates, 8 g total fat, 9 mg cholesterol, 699 mg sodium

grilled vegetables

preparation time: 25 to 30 minutes

2 to 4 red or yellow onions

2 to 4 crookneck squash, pattypan squash, or zucchini

2 to 4 slender leeks

2 to 4 red, yellow, or green bell peppers

½ cup olive oil or salad oil

2 tablespoons minced fresh herbs, such as oregano, thyme, rosemary, or tarragon (or a combination); or 2 teaspoons dry herbs

Salt and pepper

1 Peel onions and cut in half lengthwise. Trim ends from squash and cut in half lengthwise. Trim and discard root ends and any tough or wilted leaves from leeks; split leeks in half lengthwise and rinse well. Leave bell peppers whole (or cut in half, if large).

2 In a 4- to 6-quart pan, bring 2 quarts water to a boil over high heat. Add squash and leeks and boil for 2 minutes; drain, plunge into ice water, and drain again.

3 In a small bowl, stir together oil and herbs. Brush vegetables all over with oil mixture, then place on a greased grill 4 to 6 inches above a solid bed of hot coals. Cook, turning and basting often with remaining oil mixture, until vegetables are tender and streaked with brown (6 to 8 minutes for squash and leeks, 10 to 15 minutes for onions and peppers). Season to taste with salt and pepper.

makes 6 to 8 servings

per serving: 184 calories, 2 g protein, 10 g carbohydrates, 16 g total fat, 0 mg cholesterol, 7 mg sodium

indian potatoes

preparation time: about 25 minutes

1¼ pounds small red thin-skinned potatoes, scrubbed

2 tablespoons butter or margarine

1 medium-size red bell pepper, seeded and cut into thin slivers

1 medium-size onion, cut into thin slivers

1 tablespoon ground cumin

1 teaspoon ground coriander

¼ teaspoon hot chili oil, or to taste ⅓ cup chopped cilantro

½ cup nonfat sour cream

Cilantro sprigs

Salt

1 Cut potatoes crosswise into ¼-inch slices. Melt butter in a wide non-stick frying pan or wok over medium-high heat. Add potatoes, bell pepper, onion, cumin, coriander, hot chili oil, and 3 tablespoons water. Stir-fry gently until potatoes are tinged with brown and tender when pierced (about 15 minutes; do not scorch). Add water, 1 tablespoon at a time, if pan appears dry.

2 Remove pan from heat. Sprinkle potato mixture with chopped cilantro and mix gently. Spoon into a serving bowl, top with sour cream, and garnish with cilantro sprigs. Add salt to taste.

makes 4 servings

per serving: 220 calories, 6 g protein, 34 g carbohydrates, 7 g total fat, 16 mg cholesterol, 94 mg sodium

minted lettuce & peas

preparation time: about 12 minutes

1 small head red leaf lettuce, separated into leaves, rinsed, and crisped

2 tablespoons butter or margarine

1 package (10 oz.) frozen tiny peas, thawed

¼ cup chopped fresh mint or 1½ tablespoons dry mint

2 teaspoons grated lemon peel

Salt and pepper

1 Set aside 6 large lettuce leaves; cut remaining lettuce into thin strips.

2 Melt butter in a wide frying pan over medium-high heat. Add peas and lettuce strips; cook, stirring, until lettuce is wilted (about 2 minutes). Stir in mint and lemon peel. Season to taste with salt and pepper.

3 To serve, place a whole lettuce leaf on each of 6 plates. Spoon pea mixture equally into center of each leaf.

makes 6 servings

per serving: 70 calories, 3 g protein, 6 g carbohydrates, 4 g total fat, 10 mg cholesterol, 105 mg sodium

trio of sautéed mushrooms

preparation time: 30 to 35 minutes

1 ounce *each* dried cèpes (also called porcini) and dried chanterelle mushrooms (or 2 oz. *total* of either)

5 tablespoons butter or margarine

1½ pounds fresh regular mushrooms, sliced

¼ teaspoon dry thyme

Salt and pepper

1 Soak dried mushrooms in very hot water to cover for 10 minutes. Drain in a colander, rinse well with cool water, and drain again. Set aside.

2 Melt 3 tablespoons of the butter in a wide frying pan over medium-high heat. Add fresh mushrooms and cook, stirring often, until mushrooms are soft and all liquid has evaporated (10 to 15 minutes).

3 Melt remaining 2 tablespoons butter in pan. Add cèpes, chanterelles, and thyme. Cook, stirring, until mushrooms are lightly browned (about 5 minutes). Season to taste with salt and pepper.

makes 6 servings

per serving: 139 calories, 3 g protein, 11 g carbohydrates, 10 g total fat, 26 mg cholesterol, 106 mg sodium

glazed turnips

preparation time: about 15 minutes

2 cups thinly sliced turnips

2 tablespoons butter or margarine

2 tablespoons water

1 tablespoon sugar

In a wide frying pan, combine turnips, butter, water, and sugar. Cover and cook over medium-high heat, stirring often, until turnips are just tender when pierced (about 5 minutes). Uncover and continue to cook until glazed.

makes 4 servings

per serving: 80 calories, 0.6 g protein, 7 g carbohydrates, 6 g total fat, 16 mg cholesterol, 102 mg sodium

sautéed peppers & pears

preparation time: about 25 minutes

3 tablespoons butter or margarine

4 medium-size red or yellow bell peppers (or a combination), seeded and cut into ¼-inch-wide strips

3 medium-size firm-ripe pears or Golden Delicious apples, peeled, cored, and cut into ¼-inch-thick slices

¾ cup shredded jack or Münster cheese (optional)

TAKE ADVANTAGE OF PREPARED FOODS Remember, you don't have to do it all. You can take advantage of prepared foods and still personalize your menus. Go ahead and microwave a roll of ready-cooked polenta, but make your own Italian sausage and mushroom sauce to serve over it. The next time, you might cook the polenta from scratch, then serve it with a sauce from the supermarket refrigerator case. As you shop, be aware of the resources around you. Keep your eyes open for new products you can put to imaginative use in your kitchen.

1 Melt 1½ tablespoons of the butter in a wide frying pan over medium heat. Add bell peppers and cook, stirring often, until soft (about 10 minutes).

2 Melt remaining 1½ tablespoons butter in pan, then add pears. Cook, stirring often, until pears are tender when pierced (about 5 more minutes). Pour into a warm serving dish; immediately sprinkle with cheese, if desired.

makes 6 servings

per serving: 115 calories, 1 g protein, 16 g carbohydrates, 6 g total fat, 16 mg cholesterol, 60 mg sodium

spiced spinach & potatoes

preparation time: 35 to 40 minutes

¼ cup salad oil

2 large russet potatoes, peeled and cut into ½-inch cubes

¾ pound spinach, stems removed

2 cloves garlic, minced or pressed

2 teaspoons ground coriander

½ teaspoon ground ginger

About ½ cup water

1 Heat 3 tablespoons of the oil in a wide frying pan over medium-high heat. Add potatoes and cook, stirring occasionally, until browned (10 to 15 minutes). Meanwhile, rinse and drain spinach leaves; then cut crosswise into ½-inch-wide strips. Set aside.

2 Reduce heat to low. Add garlic, coriander, ginger, and remaining 1 tablespoon oil to potatoes; cook, stirring, until very fragrant (2 to 3 minutes). Pour in ½ cup of the water, cover, and simmer until potatoes are tender when pierced (about 8 minutes); add more water if needed to prevent sticking.

3 Add spinach to pan, increase heat to high, and cook, stirring, until leaves are wilted and almost all liquid has evaporated (about 2 minutes).

makes 4 servings

per serving: 242 calories, 4 g protein, 26 g carbohydrates, 14 g total fat, 0 mg cholesterol, 59 mg sodium

broccoli with rice & pine nuts

preparation time: about 35 minutes

¼ cup pine nuts or slivered almonds

2 teaspoons olive oil or vegetable oil

⅔ cup long-grain white rice

⅓ cup golden raisins

2 teaspoons chili powder

2 vegetable bouillon cubes dissolved in 2 ½ cups hot water

1¼ pounds broccoli

1 Toast pine nuts in a wide nonstick frying pan over medium-low heat until lightly browned (about 3 minutes), stirring. Remove from pan and set aside.

2 In same pan, heat oil over medium-high heat. Add rice, raisins, and chili powder. Cook, stirring, until rice begins to turn opaque (about 3 minutes). Stir in bouillon mixture; reduce heat, cover tightly, and simmer for 15 minutes.

3 Meanwhile, cut off and discard tough ends of broccoli stalks. Cut off flowerets in bite-size pieces and set aside. Thinly slice remainder of stalks.

4 Distribute broccoli flowerets and sliced stalks over rice mixture. Cover and continue to cook until broccoli is just tender to bite (7 to 10 more minutes). Mix gently, transfer to a warm serving platter, and sprinkle with pine nuts.

makes 4 servings

per serving: 247 calories, 8 g protein, 8 g total fat, 41 g carbohydrates, 0 mg cholesterol, 499 mg sodium

mediterranean squash

preparation time: about 45 minutes

2 teaspoons olive oil

1 large onion, chopped

1 pound mushrooms, thinly sliced

1½ pounds yellow crookneck squash or yellow zucchini, cut crosswise into ¼-inch slices

1½ tablespoons fresh thyme leaves or 1½ teaspoons dried thyme

3 tablespoons lemon juice

6 medium-size firm-ripe pear-shaped (Roma-type) tomatoes, cut crosswise into ¼-inch slices

½ cup thinly sliced green onions

1 ounce feta cheese, crumbled

2 oil-cured black olives, pitted and chopped

1 Heat 1 teaspoon of the oil in a wide nonstick frying pan or wok over medium-high heat. When oil is hot, add half *each* of the chopped onion, mushrooms, squash, and thyme. Stir-fry until squash is hot and bright in color (about 3 minutes).

2 Add ¼ cup water and 1½ tablespoons of the lemon juice to pan; cover and cook until vegetables are just tender to bite (about 3 minutes). Uncover and continue to cook, stirring, until liquid has evaporated (about 3 more minutes). Remove vegetables from pan and set aside.

3 Repeat to cook remaining chopped onion, mushrooms, squash, and thyme, using remaining 1 teaspoon oil; add ¼ cup water and remaining 1½ tablespoons lemon juice after the first 3 minutes of cooking.

4 Return all cooked vegetables to pan; gently stir in tomatoes. Transfer vegetables to a serving dish; sprinkle with green onions, cheese, and olives.

makes 8 servings

per serving: 78 calories, 3 g protein, 3 g total fat, 12 g carbohydrates, 3 mg cholesterol, 72 mg sodium

roasted garlic with rosemary

preparation time: about 1 hour

3 heads garlic

¼ cup extra-virgin olive oil

2 tablespoons balsamic vinegar

2 tablespoons dry wine (red or white)

1 tablespoon minced fresh rosemary leaves or crumbled dried rosemary

Salt and pepper

1 Peel garlic and put cloves in a 6- to 8-inch-wide pan.

2 Add oil, balsamic vinegar, wine, and rosemary; mix.

3 Cover and bake in a 400° oven 25 minutes. Uncover and continue to bake until garlic is light gold and soft to touch, 10 to 15 minutes longer.

4 Add salt and pepper to taste. Serve hot, warm, or at room temperature.

makes 8 servings

per serving: 105 calories, 1.8 g protein, 94 g carbohydrates, 7.1 g fat, 0 mg cholesterol, 5.1 mg sodium

roasted baby potatoes

preparation time: about 50 minutes

3 pounds thin-skinned potatoes (1½ in. wide), scrubbed

3 tablespoons olive oil

Salt and pepper

1 In a 10- by 15-inch pan, mix potatoes and oil. Lightly sprinkle with salt and pepper.

2 Roast potatoes in a 400° oven, shaking pan occasionally, until tender when pierced, 45 to 50 minutes (35 to 40 minutes in convection oven).

3 Serve potatoes hot or warm.

makes 8 servings

per serving: 182 calories, 3.3 g protein, 31 g carbohydrates, 5.4 g total fat, 0 mg cholesterol, 13 mg sodium

corn for a crowd

preparation time: about 10 minutes

12 ears corn

Butter or margarine

Salt and pepper

1 In a covered 10- to 12-quart pan over high heat, bring 5 to 6 quarts water to a boil.

2 Meanwhile, pull off and discard corn-husks and silks. Immerse ears in boiling water. Cover and cook until corn is hot, 3 to 5 minutes.

3 Drain, or lift ears from water with tongs. Season hot corn with butter and add salt and pepper to taste.

makes 12 ears

per unseasoned ear of corn: 77 calories, 2.9 g protein, 17 g carbohydrates, 1.1 g total fat, 0 mg cholesterol, 14 mg sodium

mexican rancho pinto beans

preparation time: about 30 minutes

2 firm-ripe to ripe tomatoes, rinsed, cored, and chopped

1 onion, peeled and chopped

3 fresh Anaheim chiles, rinsed, stemmed, seeded, and chopped

5 cloves garlic, peeled and chopped

6 cans (about 15 oz. *each*; 10 to 11 cups *total*) pinto beans, drained

Salt and pepper

1 In a 5- to 6-quart pan over medium-high heat, combine tomatoes, onion, chilies, and garlic. Stir often until onion is slightly browned, about 10 minutes.

2 Add beans. Cover and simmer, stirring occasionally, until hot, about 10 minutes. Season to taste with salt and pepper. Pour into a bowl.

makes 8 to 10 servings

per serving: 211 calories, 12 g protein, 39 g carbohydrates, 1.2 g total fat, 0 mg cholesterol, 793 mg sodium

refried beans with spinach

preparation time: about 40 minutes

½ pound bacon, coarsely chopped

Mexican rancho pinto beans (see above)

2 quarts spinach leaves or mustard greens, rinsed and drained

1 cup shredded Cheddar cheese

Salt and pepper

Chicken broth or water (optional)

1 In a 5- to 6-quart pan over medium-high heat, stir bacon until crisp, about 10 minutes. Lift out with a slotted spoon and drain on towels.

2 Add beans to drippings in pan; mash with a potato masher or beat with a mixer until creamy. Stir often over medium heat until hot, about 6 minutes.

3 Meanwhile, coarsely chop spinach. When beans are hot, add spinach; cover and stir occasionally, until wilted, about 3 minutes. Stir in half the cheese. Add salt and pepper to taste. If beans are not as creamy as you like, stir in a little broth. Pour into a bowl and sprinkle with remaining cheese and bacon.

makes 8 to 10 servings

per serving: 224 calories, 8.1 g protein, 9.6 g carbohydrates, 17 g total fat, 27 mg cholesterol, 419 mg sodium

curry-glazed carrots

preparation time: about 30 minutes

1 tablespoon grated orange peel

³/₄ cup orange juice

2 tablespoons maple syrup

2 teaspoons cornstarch blended with
  2 tablespoons cold water

1 teaspoon curry powder

1¼ pounds carrots, cut diagonally into
  ¼-inch slices

2 tablespoons minced parsley

Salt and pepper

1 In a bowl, stir together orange peel, orange juice, syrup, and cornstarch mixture; set aside.

2 In a wide nonstick frying pan or wok, stir curry powder over medium-high heat just until fragrant (about 30 seconds; do not scorch). Add carrots and ⅓ cup water. Cover and cook just until carrots are tender when pierced (about 4 minutes). Uncover and stir-fry until liquid has evaporated.

3 Stir orange juice mixture well; then pour into pan and cook, stirring, until sauce boils and thickens slightly. Pour carrots and sauce into a serving bowl and sprinkle with parsley. Season with salt and pepper.

makes 4 servings

per serving: 117 calories, 2 g protein, 0.4 g total fat, 28 g carbohydrates, 0 mg cholesterol, 52 mg sodium

broccoli & bell pepper with couscous

preparation time: about 30 minutes

1½ cups fat-free reduced-sodium chicken broth
  or canned vegetable broth

¼ to ½ teaspoon dried oregano

1 cup couscous

1 tablespoon pine nuts or slivered almonds

4 cups broccoli flowerets

1 teaspoon olive oil or vegetable oil

1 small red bell pepper, seeded and cut into
  thin slivers

2 tablespoons balsamic vinegar

1 In a 3- to 4-quart pan, combine broth and oregano. Bring to a boil over high heat; stir in couscous. Cover, remove from heat, and let stand until liquid has been absorbed (about 5 minutes). Transfer couscous to a rimmed platter and keep warm; fluff occasionally with a fork.

2 While couscous is standing, stir pine nuts in a wide nonstick frying pan or wok over medium-low heat until golden (2 to 4 minutes). Pour out of pan and set aside. To pan, add broccoli and ¼ cup water. Cover and cook over medium-high heat until broccoli is tender-crisp to bite (about 5 minutes). Uncover and stir-fry until liquid has evaporated. Spoon broccoli over couscous and keep warm.

3 Heat oil in pan. When oil is hot, add bell pepper and stir-fry until just tender-crisp to bite (2 to 3 minutes). Add vinegar and remove from heat; stir to scrape any browned bits from pan bottom.

4 Immediately pour pepper mixture over broccoli and couscous; sprinkle with pine nuts and serve.

makes 4 servings

per serving: 248 calories, 12 g protein, 3 g total fat, 45 g carbohydrates, 0 mg cholesterol, 278 mg sodium

cauliflower casserole

preparation time: about 25 minutes

1 cauliflower or 2 quarts cauliflower florets

1 cup whipping cream

½ teaspoon fresh-ground pepper

1½ cups shredded Gruyère cheese

Salt

1 Break cauliflower into florets, discarding core and leaves. Rinse florets.

2 In a 4- to 5-quart pan over high heat, bring about 3 quarts water to a boil. Add cauliflower and cook until just tender when pierced, 5 to 8 minutes.

3 Drain cauliflower and arrange in a shallow 1½ quart casserole.

4 Add cream to the empty pan and boil over high heat until it's reduced to ½ cup, stirring often, about 5 minutes.

5 Drizzle cream over cauliflower, sprinkle with pepper, and cover evenly with cheese.

6 Bake in a 425° oven just until cheese is lightly browned, 4 to 6 minutes. Add salt to taste.

makes 6 servings

per serving: 252 calories, 11 g protein, 5 g carbohydrates, 22 g total fat, 75 mg cholesterol, 120 mg sodium

gnocchi with sherried shallots

preparation time: about 30 minutes

2 cups thinly sliced shallots or onions

1 cup dry sherry

1½ cups nonfat sour cream

1 cup fat-skimmed chicken broth

1 package (about 18 oz.) refrigerated gnocchi

2 cups shredded skinned cooked chicken

⅓ cup chopped parsley

Fresh-grated nutmeg

Salt

1 In a 5- to 6-quart pan over high heat, stir shallots and sherry until shallots are limp, about 10 minutes.

2 Add sour cream, broth, gnocchi, chicken, and parsley. Stir until gnocchi are hot, about 5 minutes.

3 Spoon into bowls and season with nutmeg and salt to taste.

makes 4 servings

per serving: 580 calories, 36 g protein, 79 g carbohydrates, 5.3 g total fat, 71 mg cholesterol, 408 mg sodium

cheese mashed potatoes

preparation time: about 45 minutes

3 pounds russet, Yukon Gold, or thin-skinned red or white potatoes

1¼ to 1¾ cups milk or fat-skimmed chicken broth

2 to 8 tablespoons butter, regular or nonfat sour cream, cream cheese, or neufchâtel (light cream) cheese, at room temperature

Salt and pepper

1 In a covered 5- to 6-quart pan over high heat, bring 1 quart water to a boil.

2 Peel and rinse potatoes (or if desired, scrub potatoes and leave skin on). Cut potatoes into 1-inch chunks.

3 Add potatoes to boiling water, cover, and return to a boil, 3 to 4 minutes. Reduce heat to medium and simmer until potatoes mash easily, 8 to 10 minutes.

4 Meanwhile, heat milk or other liquid in a microwave-safe container in a microwave oven at full power (100%) just until steaming (don't boil). Or warm in a 1- to 1½-quart pan over medium heat.

5 Drain liquid from potatoes (save liquid if using instead of milk). Mash potatoes with a potato masher or a mixer; or press (peeled only), a portion at a time, through a ricer into another pan. Add butter or other fat, seasoning choices, and hot milk, a little at a time, and mix or beat until potatoes have desired consistency. Season to taste with salt and pepper. If potatoes have cooled, stir occasionally over low heat until hot; or warm in a microwave oven.

makes 7 or 8 servings

per serving: 172 calories, 4.2 g protein, 29 g carbohydrates, 4.4 g total fat, 13 mg cholesterol , 60 mg sodium

curried lentils & potatoes

preparation time: about 30 minutes

1 pound red thin-skinned potatoes

2 firm-ripe tomatoes

1½ cups hulled lentils such as Red Chiefs

3 cups fat-skimmed chicken broth

1 tablespoon curry powder

¼ cup finely chopped fresh mint leaves

Plain nonfat yogurt

Salt

1 Scrub potatoes and cut them into ¼-inch slices.

2 Rinse tomatoes, core, and cut each into 6 wedges.

3 In a 12- to 14-inch frying pan, combine potatoes, tomatoes, lentils, broth, and curry powder. Bring to a boil over high heat, stirring occasionally.

4 Cover pan, reduce heat, and simmer until most of the liquid is absorbed and potatoes are tender to bite, about 20 minutes, stirring occasionally.

5 Spoon into wide bowls. Sprinkle with chopped mint and add yogurt and salt to taste.

makes 4 servings

per serving: 381 calories, 29 g protein, 65 g carbohydrates, 1.3 g total fat, 0 mg cholesterol, 80 mg sodium

pasta pilaf

preparation time: about 35 minutes

1 tablespoon butter or margarine

1 large onion, finely chopped

1 clove garlic, minced or pressed

6 medium-size pear-shaped (Roma-type) tomatoes, peeled, seeded, and chopped

1 tablespoon chopped fresh basil or 1 teaspoon dried basil

8 ounces dried riso, stars, or other small pasta shape

¾ cup frozen peas

½ cup half-and-half

½ cup freshly grated Parmesan cheese

1 Melt butter in a wide nonstick frying pan over medium heat. Add onion and garlic. Cook, stirring occasionally, until onion is soft but not browned (about 5 minutes).

2 Add tomatoes, basil, and ¼ cup water; reduce heat, cover, and simmer for 10 minutes. Meanwhile, bring 8 cups water to a boil in a 4- to 5-quart pan over medium-high heat. Stir in pasta and cook just until tender to bite (8 to 10 minutes); or cook according to package directions. Drain well.

3 Add peas and half-and-half to pan with tomato mixture. Increase heat to high and bring to a boil; stir in pasta. Remove from heat and stir in ¼ cup of the cheese. Transfer to a serving dish. Add remaining ¼ cup cheese to taste.

makes 4 to 6 servings

per serving: 305 calories, 12 g protein, 9 g total fat, 45 g carbohydrates, 21 mg cholesterol, 217 mg sodium

sautéed mushrooms with apple eau de vie

preparation time: about 25 minutes

8 ounces fresh chanterelle mushrooms

8 ounces large regular mushrooms

1 teaspoon butter or margarine

4 cloves garlic, minced or pressed

1½ teaspoons chopped fresh thyme or ½ teaspoon dried thyme

About ⅛ teaspoon salt, or to taste

1 tablespoon apple eau de vie or apple brandy, or to taste

1 tablespoon cream sherry, or to taste

Thyme sprigs

Pepper

1 Rinse mushrooms and scrub gently, if needed; pat dry. Cut into ¼- to ½-inch-thick slices; set aside.

2 Melt butter in a wide nonstick frying pan or wok over medium-high heat. Add garlic and chopped thyme; stir-fry just until fragrant (about 30 seconds; do not scorch). Add mushrooms and ¼ cup water; stir-fry until mushrooms are soft and almost all liquid has evaporated (about 8 minutes). Then add salt and ¼ cup more water; stir-fry until liquid has evaporated (about 2 minutes). Add eau de vie and sherry; stir-fry until liquid has evaporated. Spoon mushroom mixture into a serving bowl and garnish with thyme sprigs. Season to taste with pepper.

makes 4 servings

per serving: 58 calories, 3 g protein, 1 g total fat, 8 g carbohydrates, 3 mg cholesterol, 84 mg sodium

pub onions

preparation time: about 60 minutes, plus 30 minutes to cool

1 ½ cups Madeira or port

¾ cup vinegar

½ cup firmly packed brown sugar

½ cup currants or raisins

⅛ teaspoon cayenne

2 pounds small white onions

3 tablespoons salad oil

Salt

1 In a 3- to 4-quart pan, combine Madeira, vinegar, sugar, currants, and cayenne. Boil rapidly, uncovered, until reduced to 1¼ cups; set aside.

2 Peel onions; arrange a single layer of onions in a 12- to 14-inch frying pan (reserve extra onions to cook in sequence). Add oil. Cook over medium-high heat until lightly browned, about 7 minutes, shaking pan to turn onions. With a slotted spoon, transfer browned onions to pan with Madeira sauce. Brown remaining onions in frying pan, then add to sauce.

3 Bring onions and sauce to a boil. Reduce heat, cover, and simmer gently; allow 10 minutes for small onions, 15 minutes for larger ones. Onions will be slightly crisp inside. Let cool; season to taste with salt. If made ahead, cover and refrigerate for up to 4 days; serve at room temperature.

makes about 4 cups

per ¼ cup: 92 calories, 1 g protein, 17 g carbohydrates, 3 g total tat, 0 mg cholesterol, 9 mg sodium

mexican rice

preparation time: about 45 minutes

1 large can (about 28 oz.) tomatoes

About 3 cups fat-free reduced-sodium chicken broth

2 teaspoons butter or margarine

2 cups long-grain white rice

1 large onion, chopped

2 cloves garlic, minced or pressed

1 small can (about 4 oz.) diced green chiles

Salt and pepper

¼ cup packed cilantro leaves

1 Drain liquid from tomatoes into a glass measure. Add enough of the broth to make 4 cups liquid. Set tomatoes and broth mixture aside.

2 Melt butter in a 4- to 6-quart pan over medium-high heat. Add rice and cook, stirring, until it begins to turn opaque (about 3 minutes). Add onion, garlic, chiles, and ¼ cup water; continue to cook, stirring, for 5 more minutes. Add more water, 1 tablespoon at a time, if pan appears dry.

3 Add tomatoes and broth mixture to pan. Bring to a boil over medium-high heat; then reduce heat, cover, and simmer until liquid has been absorbed and rice is tender to bite (about 25 minutes).

4 To serve, season to taste with salt and pepper; garnish with cilantro.

makes 10 to 12 servings

per serving: 161 calories, 4 g protein, 33 g carbohydrates, 2 g total fat, 2 mg cholesterol, 159 mg sodium

orange & rum sweet potatoes

preparation time: about 30 minutes

1 teaspoon vegetable oil

3 medium-size sweet potatoes, peeled and cut into ¼-inch-thick slices

¾ cup fat-free reduced-sodium chicken broth

½ cup orange juice

1 tablespoon rum

About 2 teaspoons honey, or to taste

2 teaspoons cornstarch

⅛ teaspoon white pepper

Salt

1 tablespoon minced parsley

1 Heat oil in a wide nonstick frying pan over medium-high heat. Add potatoes and ½ cup of the broth. Bring to a boil over medium-high heat; then reduce heat, cover, and simmer until potatoes are tender when pierced (about 10 minutes). Uncover and continue to cook, stirring occasionally, until liquid has evaporated and potatoes are tinged with brown (about 5 more minutes).

2 In a bowl, mix remaining ¼ cup broth, orange juice, rum, honey, cornstarch, and white pepper. Add cornstarch mixture to pan and bring to a boil over medium heat; boil, stirring, just until thickened. Season to taste with salt and sprinkle with parsley.

makes 4 servings

per serving: 155 calories, 2 g protein, 2 g total fat, 32 g carbohydrates, 0 mg cholesterol, 35 mg sodium

tricolor pepper sauté

preparation time: about 40 minutes

1 cup long-grain white rice

1 to 2 teaspoons sesame seeds

3 medium-size bell peppers; use 1 *each* red, yellow, and green bell pepper

1 teaspoon vegetable oil

1 small onion, cut into thin slivers

1 tablespoon minced fresh ginger

1 clove garlic, minced or pressed

1 cup bean sprouts

2 teaspoons Asian sesame oil

Reduced-sodium soy sauce or salt

1 In a 3- to 4-quart pan, bring 2 cups water to a boil over high heat; stir in rice. Reduce heat, cover, and simmer until liquid has been absorbed and rice is tender to bite (about 20 minutes).

2 Meanwhile, in a wide nonstick frying pan or wok, stir sesame seeds over medium heat until golden (about 3 minutes). Pour from pan; set aside.

3 Seed bell peppers and cut into thin slivers, 2 to 3 inches long. Heat vegetable oil in pan over medium-high heat. When oil is hot, add onion, ginger, and garlic; stir-fry for 1 minute. Add peppers; stir-fry until tender-crisp to bite (about 3 minutes). Add bean sprouts and stir-fry until barely wilted (about 1 minute). Remove from heat and stir in sesame oil.

4 Spoon rice onto a rimmed platter; pour vegetable mixture over rice and sprinkle with sesame seeds. Offer soy sauce to add to taste.

makes 4 servings

per serving: 253 calories, 5 g protein, 5 g total fat, 48 g carbohydrates, 0 mg cholesterol, 7 mg sodium

almond & zucchini stir-fry

preparation time: about 35 minutes

1 cup long-grain white rice

½ cup slivered almonds

6 large zucchini, cut into ¼- by 2-inch sticks

2 cloves garlic, minced or pressed

About 2 tablespoons reduced-sodium soy sauce

1 In a 3- to 4-quart pan, bring 2 cups water to a boil over high heat; stir in rice. Reduce heat, cover, and simmer until liquid has been absorbed and rice is tender to bite (about 20 minutes).

2 Meanwhile, in a wide nonstick frying pan or wok, stir almonds over medium heat until golden (4 to 5 minutes). Pour out of pan and set aside. To pan, add zucchini, garlic, and 2 tablespoons water. Increase heat to medium-high; stir-fry until zucchini is tender-crisp to bite and liquid has evaporated (about 9 minutes). Add 2 tablespoons of the soy sauce; mix gently.

3 To serve, spoon rice into a large bowl and pour zucchini on top of it; sprinkle with almonds. Offer more soy sauce to add to taste.

makes 6 servings

per serving: 205 calories, 7 g protein, 6 g total fat, 32 g carbohydrates, 0 mg cholesterol, 207 mg sodium

cocoa-glazed carrots & onions

preparation time: 35 to 45 minutes

10 ounces fresh pearl onions; or 1 package (about 10 oz.) frozen pearl onions

1½ pounds baby or small carrots, peeled

1 tablespoon butter or margarine

2 tablespoons lemon juice

1 tablespoon honey

1 tablespoon unsweetened cocoa powder

1 teaspoon grated fresh ginger

1 If using fresh onions, place them in a bowl and cover with boiling water. Let stand for 2 to 3 minutes. Drain; then pull or slip off skins and discard them. Also trim root and stem ends of onions.

2 Place peeled fresh onions or frozen onions in a wide nonstick frying pan. Barely cover with water and bring to a boil over high heat. Reduce heat, cover, and simmer gently until onions are tender when pierced (10 to 15 minutes). Drain onions, pour out of pan, and set aside.

3 If using baby carrots, leave whole; if using small carrots, cut diagonally into ¼-inch-thick slices. Place carrots in pan used for onions, barely cover with water, and bring to a boil over high heat. Reduce heat, cover, and simmer gently until carrots are just tender when pierced (7 to 10 minutes). Drain carrots and set aside.

4 In pan, combine butter, lemon juice, 1 tablespoon water, honey, cocoa, and ginger. Stir over medium-high heat until smooth. Add carrots and onions. Stir over high heat until sauce is thick enough to cling to vegetables (2 to 3 minutes).

makes 6 servings

per serving: 91 calories, 2 g protein, 2 g total fat, 18 g carbohydrates, 5 mg cholesterol, 61 mg sodium

italian-style swiss chard

preparation time: about 25 minutes

2½ pounds Swiss chard

2 teaspoons olive oil

2 cloves garlic, minced or pressed

2 tablespoons balsamic vinegar

1 tablespoon drained capers

1 Trim and discard discolored stem ends from chard; then rinse and drain chard. Thinly slice chard stems crosswise up to base of leaves; set aside. Use a few whole leaves to line a large platter; cover and set aside. Coarsely chop remaining leaves.

2 Heat oil in a wide nonstick frying pan or wok over medium-high heat. When oil is hot, add garlic and chard stems. Stir-fry until stems are soft (about 2 minutes). Add half the chopped chard leaves to pan, cover, and cook for 2 minutes. Add remaining leaves, cover, and cook until all leaves are wilted (about 2 more minutes).

3 Uncover pan and stir in vinegar and capers; then spoon mixture over whole chard leaves on platter.

makes 6 servings

per serving: 51 calories, 3 g protein, 2 g total fat, 8 g carbohydrates, 0 mg cholesterol, 440 mg sodium

asian-style green beans

preparation time: about 35 minutes

1 medium-size onion, chopped

8 ounces mushrooms, sliced

1 medium-size red bell pepper, cut into
   ¼-inch-wide strips

1 clove garlic, minced or pressed

3 tablespoons reduced-sodium soy sauce

1 tablespoon honey

1 pound slender green beans

¼ cup salted roasted peanuts, chopped

1 In a wide nonstick frying pan or wok, combine onion, mushrooms, bell pepper, garlic, and ¼ cup water. Stir-fry over medium-high heat until mushrooms are soft and almost all liquid has evaporated (about 10 minutes). Add water, 1 tablespoon at a time, if pan appears to be dry.

2 Stir soy sauce and honey into mushroom mixture; then transfer to a bowl and keep warm. Wipe pan clean (be careful; pan is hot).

3 To pan, add beans and ⅓ cup water. Cover and cook over medium-high heat just until beans are tender to bite (about 3 minutes). Uncover and stir-fry until liquid has evaporated.

4 Arrange beans on a rimmed serving platter; spoon mushroom mixture over beans and then sprinkle with roasted peanuts.

makes 4 to 6 servings

per serving: 118 calories, 6 g protein, 4 g total fat, 18 g carbohydrates, 0 mg cholesterol, 400 mg sodium

garlic & rosemary green beans

preparation time: about 15 minutes

¼ to ½ ounce prosciutto or bacon, chopped

1 or 2 cloves garlic, minced or pressed

1½ teaspoons chopped fresh rosemary
   or ½ teaspoon dried rosemary

1 pound slender green beans, ends removed

About ⅛ teaspoon salt, or to taste

Rosemary sprigs

Pepper

1 In a wide nonstick frying pan or wok, stir-fry prosciutto over medium-high heat just until crisp (about 1 minute). Remove from pan with a slotted spoon and set aside.

2 Add garlic, chopped rosemary, and 2 tablespoons water to pan. Stir-fry just until garlic is fragrant (about 30 seconds; do not scorch). Add beans, ⅓ cup water, and salt. Cover and cook just until beans are tender to bite (about 3 minutes). Uncover and stir-fry until liquid has evaporated. Arrange beans on a rimmed platter, sprinkle with prosciutto, and garnish with rosemary sprigs. Season to taste with pepper.

makes 4 servings

per serving: 39 calories, 3 g protein, 0.5 g total fat, 8 g carbohydrates, 2 mg cholesterol, 125 mg sodium

roasted vegetable medley

preparation time: 30 minutes
cooking time: about 45 minutes

1 large beet, peeled

2 small red thin-skinned potatoes

1 medium-size sweet potato or yam, peeled

2 large carrots

1 small red onion

5 teaspoons olive oil

2 tablespoons *each* chopped fresh oregano
   and chopped fresh basil; or 2 teaspoons *each*
   dried oregano and dried basil

1 or 2 cloves garlic, minced or pressed

¼ cup grated Parmesan cheese

Oregano and basil sprigs

Salt

1 Cut beet, unpeeled thin-skinned potatoes, and sweet potato into ¾-inch chunks. Cut carrots diagonally into ½-inch pieces; cut onion into ¾-inch wedges. Combine all vegetables in a shallow 10- by 15-inch baking pan; drizzle with oil and toss to coat vegetables evenly with oil.

2 Bake in a 475° oven until vegetables are richly browned and tender when pierced (35 to 45 minutes), stirring occasionally. Watch carefully to prevent scorching. As pieces brown, remove them and keep warm; add water, ¼ cup at a time, if pan appears dry.

3 Transfer vegetables to a platter or serving dish and sprinkle with chopped oregano, chopped basil, garlic, and a little of the cheese. Garnish with oregano and basil sprigs. Season to taste with salt and remaining cheese.

makes 6 servings

per serving: 162 calories, 4 g protein, 26 g carbohydrates, 5 g total fat, 3 mg cholesterol, 104 mg sodium

honey carrots with currants

preparation time: about 30 minutes

1½ cups water

1½ pounds large carrots, cut into
   ⅛-inch-thick, 3- to 4-inch-long sticks

2 tablespoons *each* honey and lemon juice

¼ cup dried currants

¼ cup Major Grey's chutney, minced

¼ cup orange juice

Salt

Finely slivered orange peel

1 In a 4- to 5-quart pan, bring water to a boil over high heat; add carrots, honey, and lemon juice. Cook, stirring often, until carrots are barely tender to bite (about 3 minutes). Drain carrots, reserving liquid; place carrots in a rimmed serving dish and keep warm.

2 Return cooking liquid to pan; bring to a boil over high heat. Boil, uncovered, until reduced to about ¼ cup (about 10 minutes). Add currants; stir until liquid begins to caramelize and currants look puffy. Stir in chutney. (At this point, you may let carrots and currant topping cool, then cover and refrigerate separately for up to 1 day.)

3 To serve, stir orange juice into currant topping, then spoon topping over carrots. Season to taste with salt; sprinkle with orange peel.

makes 6 to 8 servings

per serving: 108 calories, 1 g protein, 27 g carbohydrates, 0.2 g total fat, 0 mg cholesterol, 136 mg sodium

pork fried rice

preparation time: about 30 minutes

1 tablespoon vegetable oil

1 clove garlic, minced or pressed

1/2 teaspoon minced fresh ginger

1/2 cup thinly sliced green onions

4 ounces lean ground pork

8 fresh shiitake mushrooms, stems removed and caps thinly sliced

1/2 cup frozen peas

1/2 cup frozen corn kernels, thawed and drained

1/2 cup fat-free reduced sodium chicken broth

2 tablespoons reduced sodium soy sauce

3 cups cooked, cooled long grain white rice

1 Heat oil in a wide nonstick frying pan or wok over medium-high heat. When oil is hot, add garlic, ginger, and onions; then crumble in pork. Stir-fry until pork is browned (about 5 minutes).

2 Add mushrooms, peas, corn, and 1/4 cup of the broth to pan; stir-fry until liquid has evaporated (about 2 minutes). Add remaining 1/4 cup broth; then stir in soy sauce and rice. Stir-fry until rice is heated through.

makes 6 servings

per serving: 234 calories, 8 g protein, 35 g carbohydrates, 7 g total fat, 14 mg cholesterol, 282 mg sodium

red cabbage with apple

preparation time: about 10 minutes
cooking time: about 1 hour

1 tablespoon salad oil

1 large onion, thinly sliced

1 medium-size head red cabbage, shredded

1 medium-size tart apple, peeled, cored, and shredded

1 large clove garlic, minced or pressed

1 teaspoon caraway seeds

2 tablespoons firmly packed brown sugar

1/2 cup red wine vinegar

1 cup water

1 Heat oil in a wide frying pan over medium heat. Add onion and cook, stirring often, until soft (about 5 minutes). Add cabbage and apple; cook, stirring often, for 5 minutes. Stir in garlic, caraway seeds, sugar, vinegar, and water.

2 Bring cabbage mixture to a boil over high heat; then reduce heat, cover, and simmer, stirring occasionally, until cabbage is very tender to bite and almost all liquid has evaporated (about 45 minutes).

makes 4 servings

per serving: 151 calories, 3 g protein, 29 g carbohydrates, 4 g total fat, 0 mg cholesterol, 23 mg sodium

poached leeks with hazelnuts

preparation time: 50 minutes

¼ cup hazelnuts

3 slices sourdough sandwich bread, torn into pieces

2 cloves garlic, minced or pressed

¼ teaspoon dried thyme

1 teaspoon hazelnut oil or olive oil

8 medium-size leeks

Balsamic vinegar

1 Spread hazelnuts in a single layer in a shallow baking pan. Bake in a 375° oven until nuts are golden beneath skins (about 10 minutes). Let nuts cool slightly; then pour into a towel, fold to enclose, and rub to remove as much of loose skins as possible. Let cool; then coarsely chop and set aside.

2 While nuts are toasting, in a food processor or blender, whirl bread to form fine crumbs. Pour crumbs into a medium-size nonstick frying pan and add garlic and thyme. Drizzle with oil and 1 tablespoon water. Then stir over medium-high heat until crumbs are lightly browned (5 to 7 minutes). Remove from pan and set aside.

3 Trim and discard roots and tough tops from leeks; remove and discard coarse outer leaves. Split leeks lengthwise. Thoroughly rinse leek halves between layers; tie each half with string to hold it together.

4 In a 5- to 6-quart pan, bring 8 cups water to a boil over high heat. Add leeks; reduce heat, cover, and simmer until tender when pierced (5 to 7 minutes). Carefully transfer leeks to a strainer; let drain. Snip and discard strings; arrange leeks on a platter. Sprinkle with crumb mixture, then hazelnuts; offer vinegar to add to taste.

makes 4 to 6 servings

per serving: 185 calories, 5 g protein, 31 g carbohydrates, 5 g total fat, 0 mg cholesterol, 134 mg sodium

dried tomato pilaf

preparation time: 15 minutes
cooking time: 35 to 45 minutes

1 tablespoon olive oil

8 ounces portabella or button mushrooms, sliced

1 medium-size onion, chopped

1 cup long-grain white rice

2½ cups fat-free reduced-sodium chicken broth

¾ cup dried tomatoes (not packed in oil), chopped

¼ cup chopped cilantro

Salt and pepper

1 Heat oil in a 3- to 4-quart pan over medium-high heat. Add mushrooms and onion; cook, stirring often, until almost all liquid has evaporated and vegetables are lightly browned (10 to 12 minutes).

2 Add rice and stir until opaque (3 to 4 minutes). Add broth and tomatoes.

3 Bring to a boil; then reduce heat, cover, and simmer until rice is tender to bite (20 to 25 minutes). Stir in cilantro. Season to taste with salt and pepper.

makes 6 servings

per serving: 181 calories, 6 g protein, 34 g carbohydrates, 3 g total fat, 0 mg cholesterol, 280 mg sodium

roasted artichoke with vinaigrette

preparation time: 30 minutes
cooking time: about 1½ hours
chilling time: at least 2 hours

4 large artichokes

2 cups fat-free reduced-sodium chicken broth

1 teaspoon *each* **dried rosemary, dried oregano, dried thyme, and mustard seeds**

¼ cup balsamic vinegar

1 pound pear-shaped (Roma-type) tomatoes, seeded and chopped

⅓ cup sliced green onions

2 tablespoons chopped Italian or regular parsley

1 Break small, coarse outer leaves from artichokes. With a sharp knife, cut off thorny tops; with scissors, snip any remaining thorny tips from leaves. With knife, peel stems and trim bases. Immerse artichokes in water and swish up and down to rinse well; lift out and, holding by stem end, shake to remove water.

2 Place artichokes in a 9- by 13-inch baking pan. Mix broth, 1 cup water, rosemary, oregano, thyme, and mustard seeds; pour into pan. Cover very tightly with foil and bake in a 450° oven until artichoke bottoms are tender when pierced (about 50 minutes). Uncover and continue to bake until artichokes are just tinged with brown (about 8 more minutes).

3 With a slotted spoon, lift artichokes from pan. Hold briefly above pan to drain; transfer to a rimmed dish. Reserve juice in pan. When artichokes are cool enough to touch, ease center of each open; using a spoon, scoop out a few of the tiny center leaves and the choke.

4 Boil pan juices over high heat until reduced to ½ cup, about 10 minutes. Remove from heat, stir in vinegar, and pour over artichokes. Cover; refrigerate for at least 2 hours or until next day, spooning marinade over artichokes occasionally.

5 With a slotted spoon, transfer artichokes to individual plates. Stir tomatoes, onions, and parsley into artichoke marinade; spoon mixture around artichokes and into their centers.

makes 4 servings

per serving: 96 calories, 7 g protein, 19 g carbohydrates, 0.9 g total fat, 0 mg cholesterol, 441 mg sodium

sweet & sour broccoli

preparation time: about 15 minutes

About 1 pound broccoli

½ cup unseasoned rice vinegar

1 tablespoon sugar

½ teaspoon reduced-sodium soy sauce

1 Trim tough ends from broccoli stalks; peel stalks, if desired. Cut stalks into ¼-inch-thick slanting slices; cut flowerets into bite-size pieces. Arrange all broccoli on a rack in a pan above about 1 inch of boiling water. Cover and steam, keeping water at a steady boil, just until tender when pierced (5 to 8 minutes). Place broccoli in a large bowl.

2 In a small bowl, stir together vinegar, sugar, and soy sauce; pour over warm broccoli and mix well. Drain immediately and serve.

makes 4 servings

per serving: 36 calories, 2 g protein, 8 g carbohydrates, 0.2 g total fat, 0 mg cholesterol, 49 mg sodium

green & brown rice

preparation time: 25 minutes

cooking time: about 1 hour and 10 minutes

2 cups long-grain brown rice

³/₄ cup split peas

4 cups vegetable broth

2¹/₂ cups nonfat milk

2 tablespoons drained capers

¹/₂ teaspoon ground nutmeg

6 ounces fresh spinach, stems and any yellow or wilted leaves discarded, remaining leaves rinsed, drained, and finely chopped

¹/₂ cup grated Parmesan cheese

¹/₃ cup thinly sliced green onions

Whole fresh spinach leaves, rinsed and crisped

¹/₃ cup finely chopped parsley

¹/₂ cup salted roasted almonds, chopped

1 Spread rice in a shallow 3- to 3¹/₂-quart casserole, about 9 by 13 inches. Bake in a 350° oven, stirring occasionally, until rice is golden brown (about 25 minutes).

2 Meanwhile, sort through peas, discarding any debris; rinse and drain peas, then set aside.

3 In a 3- to 4-quart pan, combine 3¹/₂ cups of the broth, milk, capers, and nutmeg. Bring just to a boil over medium-high heat. Leaving casserole in oven, carefully stir broth mixture and peas into rice. Cover tightly and bake until almost all liquid has been absorbed (about 40 minutes); stir after 20 and 30 minutes, covering casserole tightly again each time.

4 Uncover casserole and stir in remaining ¹/₂ cup broth, chopped spinach, cheese, and onions; bake, uncovered, for 5 more minutes.

5 To serve, line 6 individual plates with whole spinach leaves. Stir rice mixture and spoon atop spinach; sprinkle with parsley and almonds.

makes 6 servings

per serving: 463 calories, 19 g protein, 70 g carbohydrates, 13 g total fat, 7 mg cholesterol, 1,049 mg sodium

pastina with peas

preparation time: about 35 minutes

2 ounces thinly sliced prosciutto or bacon, cut into thin strips

1¹/₂ cups dried orzo or other tiny rice-shaped pasta

1 package (about 1 lb.) frozen tiny peas

¹/₄ cup thinly sliced green onions

¹/₄ cup chopped fresh mint

¹/₄ cup olive oil

1 teaspoon finely shredded lemon peel

2 tablespoons lemon juice

Mint sprigs

Pepper

1 In a wide nonstick frying pan, cook prosciutto over medium-high heat, stirring often, just until crisp (about 3 minutes). Remove from pan and set aside.

2 In a 5- to 6-quart (5- to 6-liter) pan, bring about 3 quarts water to a boil over medium-high heat; stir in pasta and cook until just tender to bite, about 8 minutes. (Or cook pasta according to package directions.)

3 Drain rinse with cold water until cool, and drain well again. Pour pasta into a large serving bowl; add peas, onions, and chopped mint. Mix gently.

4 In a small bowl, beat oil, lemon peel, and lemon juice until blended. Add to pasta mixture; mix gently but thoroughly. Sprinkle with prosciutto and garnish with mint sprigs. Season to taste with pepper.

makes 6 servings

per serving: 364 calories, 14 g protein, 52 g carbohydrates, 12 g total fat, 8 mg cholesterol, 282 mg sodium

asparagus with garlic crumbs

preparation times: 40 minutes

3 slices sourdough sandwich bread,
  torn into pieces

2 teaspoons olive oil

2 cloves garlic, minced or pressed

36 thick asparagus spears, tough ends
  snapped off

Salt and pepper

1 In a blender or food processor, whirl bread to form fine crumbs. Pour crumbs into a wide nonstick frying pan; add oil and garlic. Cook over medium-high heat, stirring often, until crumbs are lightly browned (5 to 7 minutes). Remove from pan and set aside.

2 Trim ends of asparagus spears so that spears are all the same length (reserve scraps for soups or salads). For the sweetest flavor and most tender texture, peel spears with a vegetable peeler.

3 In frying pan, bring about 1 inch water to a boil over medium-high heat. Add a third of the asparagus and cook, uncovered, until just tender when pierced (about 4 minutes). Lift from pan with a slotted spoon and place in a bowl of ice water to cool. Repeat with remaining asparagus, cooking it in 2 batches.

4 Drain cooled asparagus well; then arrange on a large platter, Sprinkle with crumb mixture; season to taste with salt and pepper.

makes 8 servings

per serving: 70 calories, 5 g protein, 11 g carbohydrates, 2 g total fat, 0 mg cholesterol, 68 mg sodium

roasted potatoes & carrots with citrus dressing

preparation time: about 15 minutes
baking time: 35 to 45 minutes

Citrus Dressing (page 155)

2 pounds small red thin-skinned potatoes,
  scrubbed and cut into 1-inch chunks

4 teaspoons olive oil or salad oil

4 medium-size carrots, cut into 1-inch chunks

Salt and pepper

Basil sprigs

1 Prepare Citrus Dressing; refrigerate.

2 In a lightly oiled 10- by 15-inch rimmed baking pan, mix potatoes with 2 teaspoons of the oil. In another lightly oiled 10- by 15-inch rimmed baking pan, mix carrots with remaining 2 teaspoons oil. Bake potatoes and carrots in a 475° oven, stirring occasionally, until richly browned (35 to 45 minutes); switch positions of baking pans halfway through baking.

3 In a shallow bowl, combine potatoes, carrots, and Citrus Dressing. Serve hot or warm. Before serving, season to taste with salt and pepper; garnish with basil sprigs.

makes 6 to 8 servings

per serving: 176 calories, 3 g protein, 35 g carbohydrates, 3 g total fat, 0 mg cholesterol, 66 mg sodium

index